SURVIVING SILENCE

Thank you for the work you do in the world!

SHEREE TRASK

ISBN: 978-1-951503-88-8 (Hardcover)
ISBN: 978-1-951503-89-5 (Paperback)
ISBN: 978-1-951503-90-1 (Ebook)

Authorsunite.com

Trigger Warning—Please Read

Throughout this book there are several mentions of my personal experience with rape, as well as conversations around many forms of trauma. If you feel triggered by any of the content within this book, please take a break and come back when you feel grounded and ready to do so. If at any time you feel vulnerable or in need of immediate support, I encourage you to seek help from a professional or someone you trust to hold your truth with care.

RAINN, the National Sexual Assault Hotline,
can be reached at 1-800-656-HOPE (4673).
The National Domestic Violence Hotline can be reached
at 1-800-799-SAFE (7233).

You don't have to face it alone.

Dedication

To the Universe for placing every single person and experience in my path, including the heartbreaking and often confusing lessons to navigate—*thank you.*

To all the women who have stood in the fire alongside me, shoulder to shoulder—*thank you.*

To all the women who went before me, paving the way to show us all the power of resilience, courage, and using our voice for good to create massive change in the world—*thank you.*

To all the men who've set a beautiful example of unshakable integrity and conscious masculinity while providing a safe environment for us to show up and be seen—*thank you.*

To the best friends a girl could ask for, for holding me, supporting me and loving me through each piece of my evolution with compassion and grace—*thank you.*

To my beautiful Nana for showing me that the desires of our heart are only made possible by vulnerably and honestly embracing our truth and living in alignment with our highest and best, each and every day—*thank you.*

And to my biggest cheerleader, my incredible mom, for encouraging me and believing in me...even when I doubted my dreams (and healing) were possible—*thank you.*

Contents

Introduction: The Question

"Wanna fly, you got to give up the shit that weighs you down."
– Toni Morrison, Song of Solomon

Trauma has been a part of my personal experience even before I was born. Having a drug and alcohol-addicted biological father, whom I never knew, didn't help matters. Nor did having a stepfather I loved dearly leave and never speak to me again after he and my mom divorced, bits of which I will share throughout this book.

There was also the incident with my fourth grade music teacher whom I vividly remember following me into the dark music closet after practice and setting me on his lap as he stroked my face, telling me how beautiful I was and pointing out that my rosy cheeks matched my pink shirt perfectly. Even at 10 years old, I knew it was wrong. So much so that I stormed out of the closet and ran straight to the principal's office to tell an adult what had happened. I don't know what happened to my teacher after that, likely nothing. But I do know that I never played the violin again. I created an association that playing music wasn't safe, and instead I dove into sports, making the excuse that *the violin was boring*. And while I'm sure there was some truth to that, underneath the excuses was fear and the very real feeling that I was going to need to figure out how to protect myself from the world to feel safe, even from the adults I believed I was supposed to trust.

Fast forward to 1999 when I graduated high school and followed my dream of moving from a small town outside of Seattle to San Diego, completely alone. I managed to get a job at a local shop near my house, and within weeks my (much older) boss began regularly harassing me, making inappropriate comments about my body while sharing his wild fantasies. When I told the owners, he barely got a slap on the wrist. I quit.

Then there was the big kahuna of them all. Just a year later, I reluctantly said yes to going on a date with someone I'd had a bad feeling about, after months of persistence on his part.

I was 19 years old.

That night would change me in more ways than I can possibly explain in these pages. But beyond changing me, it allowed me to become more of myself and see the experience for what it was—an intervention in the life I was trying to *forcefully create*, instead of learning to accept and find gratitude for the life that was truly meant for me.

I know it's not easy to see what's possible when we're deep in our shit. For many of us, our traumas, both old and new, are held deep inside, unconsciously playing pinball between our bodies, hearts and psyches. Throughout this book, I will be offering you an invitation into acceptance (not to be confused with making what happened okay), as well as providing you with tools to focus on better feeling states, inevitably cultivating better feeling outcomes. Overcoming our setbacks takes work if we want to truly heal, which I believe we all do. I will share how we can get beyond our traumas by sharing insights that have helped me, as well as many others I know and love. Things I believe can help you on your healing journey, too.

When Intuition Screams

It was October 15, 2000, when my world as I knew it changed forever. It was the night my innocence was shattered, and no matter how hard I tried, I would never be the person I once was. That night, before our "date" even began, the man I agreed to go out with raped me, and I chose to stay silent...*for three-and-a-half years.* Subsequently, I spent years in and out of the hospital after having endured not only a violating assault, which nobody knew about, but also the experience of that fateful night resulting in an ectopic pregnancy.

It's strange for me to think about all the experiences I have had in my life involving trauma, and yet I still feel strongly that each traumatic moment became a defining point in my life that was *for* me in some way, instead of against me. In fact, every question I pose throughout this book is an invitation for you to ask yourself a similar question on your journey home to yourself. Because I promise you, even if you can't see it now or you think it's total bullshit to think that a horrendous experience could possibly be *for* your benefit, my experience has been that what is available on the other side of trauma can actually be quite beautiful.

Trauma comes in many forms—all of which are valid, real, and personal. Whether it's childhood abuse, rape, being groped on the subway, emotional abuse by a parent or partner, loss of a loved one, illness, accidents...you name it! Trauma is not linear, nor is it an enjoyable experience.

Despite all the chaos I've endured, much of which I'm sure you will be able to relate to in some way, I am a firm believer that as a whole, the world is a safe and loving place, mainly because I have chosen this story, which I will get into later. I truly believe there's a deeper reason for every experience we encounter and if you let it, you may just find that the blessings hiding within all the shit have actually been there all along. (That's why I say difficult events happen *for* you, but more on that later.)

I'm going to bare my soul to you in the pages to come. Sure, part of sharing my stories is about my own continuous healing journey, but on a larger scale, this book is for you. I've chosen to step into my own vulnerability to empower *you* with tools and inspiration for hope and healing. This book is about bringing you back to your true essence and reminding you of your innate power. It's about highlighting your strengths, despite what's happened in your life. And coming home to the warrior within that's still standing, reading these words now.

Sharing my experiences of trauma connects me deeply with my purpose, which is to be a voice and take a stand for those not yet ready or possibly too afraid to speak. People like you, like me, like us! Whatever you've been through, please know that I see you, I honor you, and you are not alone.

As a survivor of many forms of trauma, I understand the fear, the confusion, the anger, the sadness, the grief, the silence, the stories we create based on something that happened that we didn't choose. I can also assure you that healing is possible, if you allow change to change you, and you embrace the new version of you—*the one who survived, the you that can and will thrive.*

The *you* that exists here and now is different. This version of you will likely require more care, compassion and love… *from yourself.* The new, maybe a bit unfamiliar version staring back at you every time you look in the mirror is as valuable as the person that existed before the trauma occurred. Different doesn't have to be bad. It can simply be…*different.* How you got to this place may be out of your control, but what you do with your experiences is entirely up to you.

Let me remind you that you, sweet soul, are divine. You are perfectly imperfect. Your beautiful heart deserves to be loved and honored and adored. Your scars are what make you *you.* And while I know all too well that sometimes the pain, fear and doubt can seep out like a leaky faucet looking to drown your spirit, you are too strong to go down without a fight.

I see you, because I am you. I know your soul, just as you know mine. And we are resilient beyond our wildest imagination both alone and together.

I could have chosen to be a victim. Trauma is fucked up and there is no right way to handle it. But labeling myself as a "victim" wasn't how I was raised, and staying in a place of helplessness didn't feel authentic to me. Yet in the same breath, my trusty pride took a front seat when I was raped and instead of sharing my truth to prevent him from doing this to someone else, I chose to work through the emotions *on my own* and deal with the aftermath that this unfathomable situation triggered, alone. Maybe you've hidden your story deep inside, keeping it all to yourself as a means of self-preservation. Either way, I want to remind you that your process is yours and whatever it looks like, it's okay.

While your experiences may not have been your fault, healing is your responsibility. How you choose to heal begins and ends with you. You *do* have the power to create a new story, no matter where you've been or what you've been through.

My story is not uncommon. My hope is that by sharing my story, I can shed light on the reality of trauma, and some of the ways in which it shows up, and I can offer even a small amount of healing to the collective because...this all-too familiar story? It's gotta stop! My wish is that you will allow yourself to dig deep and find the courage within to not only do whatever it takes to heal but to keep going in spite of your past.

The little voice that tells you silence is the answer is, in my experience, wrong. And if you're afraid of judgment or pity, well, my dear, welcome to the club. Fear, while a real and valid emotion, too easily becomes a story we tell ourselves as a way to avoid showing up and being brave with our life. You don't need to shout from the rooftops, but hiding your truth from yourself, above all else, is damaging and unsupportive to not only you but to those you love.

When we band together as survivors, we create an opportunity to rise as the courageous souls we are, standing shoulder to shoulder as we work to shift consciousness so that people don't have to feel the depth of this pain anymore. We are not objects. We are brave warriors that made it out alive, and we deserve to be free from the pain—that includes releasing any stories we're holding onto that may be keeping us stuck in a cycle of shame, sadness and struggle. In their place, we can then grant ourselves permission to tell ourselves a new, more empowering story—one that supports how far we've come and where we've still yet to go.

I am not that old narrative that kept me trapped in silence, paralyzed by my desire to remain the same after experiencing trauma—and you don't have to be your old story either. You're everything good in this world. And you are far more powerful than you could possibly imagine. It's time to break the silence. It's time to speak up, in whatever way feels true and safe. It's time to shift. It's time to connect and reclaim your power. It's time to live unapologetically, as the version of *you* that has emerged from the pain as you realize you are valuable because you exist. Let that be enough, because you're more than enough.

You may be reading this now thinking, "*I've never been raped so how does this apply to me?*"

It's simple.

As I mentioned, trauma comes in many forms. Rape is only one of the ways in which it shows up. But think about the myriad of other ways trauma is expressed and, ultimately, how that single (or continual) event has shaped you.

Cat calls. Molestation. Snarky inappropriate remarks disguised as *compliments*. Uninvited sexually explicit dialogue. Rape. Grooming as children. Passive-aggressive partners who make you feel on top of the world one day, only to make you feel like trash the next. Gaslighting—someone telling you your genuine emotions aren't valid for reasons that make you constantly second-guess yourself. Microaggressions we've been told to ignore or pass off as "joking." The list goes on and on.

The truth is, you will never be the same person you were before the event(s) and that deserves to be acknowledged. Even celebrated—because the *you* who survived is far too bold and brave to play small. There is an overarching trauma happening in our world that has demanded silence, from women in particular. From a young age so many girls are told they're "to be seen and not heard." They're praised for being demure and quietly accepting of whatever harshness or scraps the world dishes out to us. It reminds me of *The Great Gatsby*, when Daisy tells her daughter, "I hope she'll be a little fool. That's the best thing a girl can be in this world, a beautiful little fool." Almost 100 years after Fitzgerald wrote that (1925), we're still fighting that expectation in 2022. And that's only one example of the conditioning we've had imprinted, whether personally or through generations before us.

As women, many of us have shut down. We've made silent and afraid our normal. We've allowed societal expectations to cloud the truth that we are fierce and free and fundamentally necessary to creating a greater oneness for humanity and everything beyond.

Women: the most sacred creation on the planet. The bringers of life. The nurturers. The mothers. The divine manifestation of feminine grace, softness, beauty, sensuality and desire.

Let us be silent no more, my sisters. Together we fall, together we rise. This is a new era for our spirits to soar. Together in sisterhood, guiding one another toward the ultimate truth—we are *love.* It's time to get into the practice of having infinite love for ourselves so that we may pour that same love into humanity and the world as a whole, as we show up in our perfectly imperfect messiness.

It is not our job to conform to make others comfortable.

We deserve better than that!

If you want to create change then sometimes that means you've gotta shake things up. And always, it takes courage.

What you have to say matters. So when you question your worth or your purpose on this planet, know that there is a reason you were given a voice. There is a reason you were given free will and thought and every experience you've encountered.

Nothing is by accident. And if hearing that triggers you, then I would encourage you to ask yourself *why*. Because everything, on some level, is a choice—even the emotions you're feeling right now as you think of all the bullshit you've been through that you've been holding onto and allowing to take up space in your life.

Brave one, it's time to let go of it all.
Your past.

Other people's expectations.
Negative self-talk.
The victim mentality.
Your lack of self-worth, self-love, self-respect.
The judgment.

And it's time to harness the power within so that you can create a new story you're proud of. A story that inspires you to do more, be more, love more.

It's time. And it's yours for the taking.

We need you. What you've been through matters. Who you are *matters.* And you are so incredibly worthy of having it all.

No matter where you've been, know that there is a way out. It starts with accepting your past, embracing your experiences, choosing the lessons within and using them to propel you forward while loving yourself unconditionally.

I see you, because I am you.

And I love you, as you are.

The Road Ahead

In the pages to follow, each chapter is titled with a question, which will be posed again for you to ponder at the end. I have also compiled all of these questions in the back of the book in a *Companion Journal,* in case it further supports your process. These are the big questions that I asked myself (more than once) on my own healing journey, and I have little doubt that these questions will align with your own experience walking this road back home to yourself, too.

While it's no secret that each of our journeys are individual, there is a collective power that happens when we dive in together, get honest about where we've still yet to heal, and decide to do the work to come out stronger than we thought possible. Yes, this journey is yours. But it's also all of ours. Because when we heal ourselves, we heal pieces of the whole. And that's how we all come home, back to what matters—*our truth*, scars and all.

I've poured my heart into the content in each chapter with the intention to highlight the overarching message I want you to really embody: *You are not alone and you are not bad, wrong, or broken because of your traumas.* No matter what pain you've been through in the past, healing is your birthright. You are capable. You are worthy. You are enough. No matter where you are now or where you want to go, you can do this. And I'm here to hold you through the proverbial birth canal as you step into a fresh way of living, loving, and leading—for yourself and others who are brave enough to follow your example of strength, power, and resilience.

I will be posing some hard questions while offering my own point of view on each, providing exercises for you to implement as you'd like, and offering mindset shifts to get you back on track when you feel like you've been derailed. This book will be a loving kick in the ass as you navigate what feels good and true and nourishing on your path to freedom and personal power. And while I will be cheering you on throughout, and encouraging your progress as well as helping you to manage the pitfalls, the journey back home is squiggly at best and certainly not for the faint of heart.

I intentionally refrained from adding stats to this book so as not to highlight the prevalence of trauma (although the numbers are staggering and quite heartbreaking). Instead, I've chosen to highlight the healing that's possible, in spite of these unfortunate experiences, in hopes of inspiring more people to come forward, however they see fit, and commit to moving through the pain and into the joy that's available on the other side of silence.

I have also chosen to use the gender terms she/her/woman within these pages, as that is what I personally identify/ connect with. However, this book is for any and all survivors (and their loved ones) looking for hope and inspiration, no matter your gender expression and/or identification.

Healing encompasses all the emotions, both the positive and not-so-great alike. But that's also the beauty of facing our humanness head on...and we cultivate those results by taking one step forward, then another, and another... and so it goes.

The questions are simple, although really feeling into the answers takes a level of compassion and vulnerability that may feel incredibly hard and scary to stay present to in the moment. Allow yourself to be in this space. Use the tools within these pages to support your own journey as you adapt what's no longer serving you and then step into the *you* that's longing to be free.

I will give you my answers to the questions asked chapter by chapter. But it's up to *you* to find the answers that resonate deep within and leave you feeling at peace, ready to step over the threshold into the beautiful unknown.

By the end of this book, my hope is that you will understand on a deeply intuitive level that you are safe to take up whatever space you need to come into your own strength and wholeness. We need you and your courage. And we need your voice, now more than ever.

Let's continue healing together, shall we?

Onward we go, warriors.

Sheree

1

Why Me?

"Somewhere between what she survived, and who she was becoming, was exactly where she was meant to be. She was starting to love the journey and find comfort in the quiet corners of her wildest dreams. They say people don't change.... Well, she wasn't always this way. Even if she didn't change the entire world, she would change her part of it. And she would affect the people she shared it with. A butterfly whose wings have been touched, can indeed still fly. Whether something was meant to be, or meant to leave, didn't matter as much anymore. She would soak up the sun, kiss the breeze, and she would fly regardless."
– J. Raymond

The moment I shut my car door, I knew I had a choice.

My heart was racing, my breath had become almost nonexistent. The sound of rain on my windshield, a reminder of my tear-soaked cheeks. I felt the heaviness suffocating my airways, filling the space of my entire being with nothingness.

I had to pull myself together. My roommate couldn't know what had just happened. Nobody could know.

Walking through the doorway that had welcomed me in only a short time earlier now dumped me out like a piece of trash after being violated and dismissed. My feet felt heavy as if I was traversing through quicksand as my cold, shaking hands reached for my keys feeling blindly around in my purse—my fingers numb, just as my heart now felt. As I worked to consciously connect to my breath, the physical and emotional pain of what had just happened welled in my eyes while my mind tried to protect me by dissociating from the reality of the situation. Nothing felt real—not even me.

My entire body was on high alert. I could still feel the pressure of his manhood between my legs as the fatigue from fighting began to set in, consuming every part of my fragile body. My knees began to wobble, begging to collapse as I whispered to myself, *one foot in front of the other* on repeat as I made my way to my car. I felt like a zombie—dead and yet, still very much alive.

My mind swirled with a myriad of emotions from fear to anger to disappointment to frustration to sadness—until I had nothing left. I felt like a shell of a woman—raw, numb and in absolute shock. *How could this have happened? I should've trusted my intuition when it screamed at me not to go. I should've rejected his invitation and stayed home tonight.* I "should-have'd" all over myself, opening the floodgates to the deepest, most visceral pain I have ever known. He took pieces of me that night that I knew would never return.

Walking away from the unimaginable, I felt incomplete, as if my limbs had been removed and I was trying to run a marathon without legs or prosthetics. How would I continue to live as *me* when I was no longer whole, now merely a shell of who I used to be before that monster decided he would try to break me?

This would become the most pivotal moment in my life—even now, looking back. The girl that pulled up to that house in her silver Volkswagen Jetta, without a care in the world, had just walked out of that same house a completely different woman. Shattered. Terrified. Alone. And determined to rise.

You will not break me. I won't let you.

I remember these thoughts as if it were yesterday. They are still raw, my emotions still tied to the memory of an innocence lost and a life that would never again be the same.

But life has a funny way of giving us exactly what we never knew we needed. Heartache. Abuse. Loss. And then there are the moments where we actually feel as if we are being divinely guided and supported.

It all comes down to perspective—how we choose to see our experiences…as traumas or as blessings. It's about keeping the faith and trusting that things happen *for* us, even when it feels as if the world is against us. Even the things that may appear terrible to the outside world.

That would easily become the most terrifying night of my life. What started as an invitation to his house to grab a jacket before a movie quickly turned into a fight for my life.

As I walked through the door, his nearly 200 pound frame grabbed me. And as he lifted me up and softly kissed my lips, his sensual demeanor quickly turned aggressive. I begged him to stop, but he wouldn't let me go.

"Stop! Please stop!"

But he was bigger than me. He was stronger than me. And as he picked me up and threw me on his bed, he pulled down my pants as I began to sob, begging him to let me go. My body went into protection mode and I blacked out, only remembering glimpses of the worst night of my life.

There are moments I remember as if it were yesterday. Like the way he smelled of cologne and aftershave. Or the way his hot breath felt vile against my neck. Or the way he stared into my eyes with such hatred and malice that I felt as if the Devil himself was penetrating me with a force greater than I had ever known.

I also remember the way my nails dug into his back as the exhaustion kicked in and my eyes closed, praying for it to end so I could go back to my life.

He raped me that night.

I was now a stereotype. #metoo

I was 19. I was not on birth control, and I had only had sex with one person in my life prior to that night.

I didn't ask for this. I didn't agree to this. I didn't want this. But he didn't care.

As he finished, he stood up proudly, buttoned his pants with a smirk on his face and said, "See baby, I told you

you'd like it." And he walked out of the room like nothing had happened. As if he hadn't just violated me, leaving me alone in my pain, both physical and emotional.

As I sunk further into his bed, my legs, exhausted from fighting, hung off the side with my jeans wrapped around my ankles and my shirt torn down the middle. I felt the tears streaming uncontrollably down my cheeks…my throat constricting the breath that wanted to spill out as I began to comprehend the enormity of what had just happened. And it was at that moment that I had a feeling of sheer panic wash over me. *How could I hide this? How could I possibly keep this secret?*

I slid off his bed, fell to my knees and crawled into the bathroom adjacent to where he'd obliterated my trust and safety. I sat on the floor sobbing and praying for this all to be a bad dream. I remember standing up and looking in the mirror at my tear-soaked cheeks, makeup smeared down my face and thinking, *Who is this girl looking back at me?*

I was staring at a stranger, unrecognizable in appearance, with a soul burning hot…but for what? I wasn't sure. I didn't even know if I wanted to get to know her…this *new version* of me. But I knew I didn't want to stay here, trapped in a room that was now a prison of secrets and suffering.

I mustered all the energy I had left to put myself back together. I pulled up my pants, clenched my ripped shirt over my breasts, and blinked away tears from my empty eyes. With mascara running down my face and a parched mouth begging for water, I took a deep breath and walked straight out of his bedroom, past the living room where he sat comfortably on his sofa and out his front door without a word.

As soon as the door shut behind me, I heard my Nana's voice in my head: "*Whatever you do with this experience is up to you, little one.*" At 19, I knew about the power of choice—in my thoughts, words and actions. My Nana had taught me that, and I wouldn't let her down.

I sat in my car for what felt like forever, unable to move. It was in that eerie stillness of time that I asked the Universe to protect my heart and find a way to forgive him so I could move on with my life. I don't know how long I sat there on the side of the road, listening to the rain beat down on my windshield. But that moment would become the most important moment of my life, even as I write this book, decades later. I refused to drive home until I could find some semblance of peace—until my heart could accept that "hurt people, hurt people," and this act of violation was not about me at all, it was about him and *his* pain. I was merely a vessel to pour that pain into.

I forgave him the same night he raped me. Which ironically, as it turns out, was the easy part. The real struggle would be in forgiving myself for staying silent about it for three-and-a-half years afterward. During that time, I couldn't help but wonder if he had done this again to someone else, a thought that gutted me and sent me down a spiral of conviction to do whatever was necessary to prove that I deserved to be here, no matter the cost.

I realize that this may seem absurd. And I understand that according to everyone else I have ever met that's been through anything similar to my experience, forgiveness is often the *last* step in their journey (if it ever happens). But I wasn't raised that way and to be fair, doing whatever possible to move forward was all that I knew, which included what felt right for me in that moment which was to forgive the man that raped me, and find a way to create something beautiful from this incomprehensible experience.

I want to be crystal clear here...

Forgiving him wasn't *for him*—**it was for me.** Forgiving him meant peace in *my* heart. Forgiving him gave me the space I needed to find freedom in my pain and see another perspective. I chose to see this as a blessing, despite not understanding *why* it happened. And although I felt more raw than I had in my entire life, I knew I needed to find a way to use this as fuel to create something better.

As I drove home in a daze...shaken and trembling, I made a conscious decision to release my anger, as I pressed my foot on the gas pedal and ugly cried all the way home. I refused to let him take any more of my power. Not then, not ever. What happened had already changed me. And while I didn't know it at the time, it would also provide clarity around my role in the world and the work I was put here to do.

I would soon come to realize that this was only the beginning.

You've Gotta Be Kidding Me

It was just three weeks later that I ended up in Urgent Care with terrible stomach pain. I'd just worked a 12-hour shift at the salon (for the third day in a row) and thought that maybe it was exhaustion setting in, possibly along with a stomach bug. But the pain was intense and unlike anything I'd ever felt before, which had me doubled over, feeling nauseous and dizzy.

When a room finally opened up for me, I put on one of those flattering hospital gowns as the nurse proceeded to do an exam and ordered a few tests in hopes of getting to the bottom of this pain. UTI? Appendicitis? Ulcer? I spent about an hour waiting in agony, which felt like an eternity, before I got the news. When she finally re-entered my room, she had the doctor in tow.

"So, good news! It looks like you're healthy." Pause. "And I'm not sure if this is good news or not, but it looks like you're pregnant…just about three weeks along." Silence.

Stunned, I couldn't breathe. I began gasping for air as the unfiltered words fell out of my mouth. "Get it out of me! Get it out now!"

The confusion, shock and utter disbelief blasted through me. How was this real? Surely I was in a real-life nightmare. This could not actually be happening, could it?

Distraught and devastated, I called my roommate—who happened to be my childhood best friend from back home—and told her to come immediately. I reluctantly revealed to her that I was pregnant, while I kept the story behind how this little life came to be a secret. As she tried to soothe my worry, I became frantic and emotional, sobbing as fear bubbled up, leaving my body shaking. And once again, I blacked out.

This pregnancy, along with the rape, became my big, scary secret. And although I was terrified and beside myself, I was determined to give it purpose…*alone.* This was all part of my new story, the one I still had yet to accept and embrace. I would not tell a soul about the man who raped me or the circumstances that had created an innocent life within me (aside from sharing the smallest of details with my roommate). I would pretend that everything was okay...that *I* was okay. I would continue along with college, crush my goals and prove to myself (and the world) that I was worthy and enough, still capable of achieving all the things I'd dreamed of attaining. Although deep down, I wasn't actually sure my dreams were possible anymore. If I kept telling myself everything was fine, surely the Universe would reward me for my courage and bravery. If I could just overcome this, anything was possible. Right...?

For the next few years, I suffered in silence. Not because I felt any sense of guilt or shame about what had happened (I actually didn't), but because I didn't want to be seen as *different.* I wanted people to still see me as the strong, independent girl who seemingly had her shit together. I didn't want pity or to hear the all-too-common phrase, "I'm so sorry to hear about what happened to you..." I just wanted things to go back to the way they were and leave this nightmare behind me.

Maybe you can relate to hiding. Or staying quiet out of fear or shame or guilt, or whatever emotion is tied to your own silence...to your secrets.

A lot of the women I've spoken to have told me they don't want to bother anyone, or hurt their family. Many people are afraid of what others will think, how they will be perceived (weak, damaged, broken). My response to all of that is always the same... *But what about you? What about your heart, your soul, your needs, your feelings, your healing?*

Because the truth is, we cannot control others' reactions or emotions toward a given situation. It is up to us to figure out what we need, *for ourselves,* in order to heal.

It's in the process of choosing ourselves that we are able to show others that it's possible to come out on the other side—happy, healthy and whole. You will be different, there's no doubt about that. And in my experience, these things—although less than ideal—can be the greatest gift you've ever received.

It'll take time. It won't be easy. It will likely be messy and uncomfortable. But you are worth the effort to get on the other side of the pain and begin to live again.

I understand wanting things to just remain the way they were before the trauma occurred. For me that was living life as a college co-ed in a beautiful beach town, surrounded by friends and fun—carefree and ready to take on the world. Your "before" may be similar, or entirely different. Either way, things will never be the same as they were *then*...they can't be! And you can't expect yourself to be the same, either.

So often we think that if we just follow the rules, by *society's standards*—go to school, get a job, marry a "good enough" partner, buy a house, have well-adjusted children—everything will work out on our terms, and we'll be shooting rainbows out of our asses in no time. It's a cute idea, but it's also ridiculous. We try so desperately to fit ourselves into a mold of what we believe will make us happy...what society tells us will make us happy. And, in turn, we fail to plan for the unexpected. But when we become rigid in how we experience life, always following the rules as they are and refusing to adapt to unforeseen circumstances, the unexpected events are that much more of a punch to the gut when things don't go our way.

Insert: The Universe

She's always there, often shaking her head at our unwillingness to relinquish control. In moments like these, we often find ourselves looking up to the heavens thinking something like, "*What the actual fuck?!*"

And we either break or we conquer.

Maybe we do both.

But as I'm sure you know by this point in your life, you can't always control the outcome. It's in the art of surrender that flow shows up and when that happens, your constant fight against life turns into freedom and your pain becomes your power.

Deep down, I didn't want the pregnancy or the memory that would be tied to my sexual assault. I even attempted to have an abortion, which didn't work. And as divine intervention would have it, I got a call from the nurse the day after my attempted termination to review my follow-up bloodwork. Her voice was urgent.

"Sheree, we need you to come in right now, it's important."
"Can you just tell me over the phone? I'm not feeling well, and I have guests in town." Standard teenager response.
"Sheree, this is serious. If you don't come in right now... well...(long pause)...you could die." Great bedside manner.
"What do you mean? What's going on?" Shock.

"It's ectopic. That means, you're still pregnant. If we don't handle this now... Listen, I just need you to come in immediately. We can talk about your options in person." Fear.

After throwing up in the bathroom and putting on my, "everything's fine" face, I asked my roommate to give me a ride to the doctor, giving her no information other than, "something's off with my bloodwork."

Thank God for best friends.

The Choice

I was given two options. Option one: have surgery to remove the ectopic pregnancy, which was lodged in one of my fallopian tubes. Or option two: go through a series of weekly "chemo" injections to allow the pregnancy to pass "naturally." Option two was apparently the better choice given my age, as it provided a lower risk of complications and it would be more likely that my fallopian tubes would remain healthy should I choose to have children someday.

Either way, I couldn't keep the pregnancy. Because it was ectopic, I had to choose one or the other, and quickly.

"So what will it be?" She was so matter of fact.

I mean, this wasn't like she was asking me if I wanted pizza or tacos. I was being asked to make a really scary decision, that I didn't quite understand, after a traumatic experience that nobody knew about.

"Can I have a minute?" At which point, she quietly left the room.

I let the tears flow as I sat with the news. I thought about my life. My dreams. My secret. Then I took a deep breath before deciding on option two. And from November 2000 through February 2001, I became a regular patient at UCSD Medical Center in San Diego, CA for weekly injections straight into my buttcheek.

While controversial, for me this felt like a blessing. For years I wondered if that was my one shot at motherhood. But I know it happened exactly the way it was meant to. And as hard as it was to face it all alone (by choice), it was through grieving and processing the pain and confusion that I gave it all purpose. I chose to view that experience with a whole new meaning. It was in my mess that I committed to turning all of this into my mission to create a life where I could truly live...

Unapologetically out loud.

My calling to support others with their voice, their story, their message had found me. But my journey was far from over. The next decade or so would prove to be challenging in its own right, showing me the power our secrets hold to keep us sick, which I will dive into in a bit.

Breaking My Silence

The night that I shared my story for the first time, I was on a second date with a man that I would end up dating for 11 years. It was three-and-a-half years after my assault, a very different date than the one I would be telling him about, which began and ended with my attacker assaulting me. I can't say exactly how I knew it was time to break my silence because I didn't go into our second date with the intention to do so. Somehow, though, my soul knew it was time to let it go...whether I felt ready or not.

As we sat together on my oversized chaise lounge in my quaint one-bedroom apartment in Coronado, CA with a glass of wine, getting to know each other and laughing hysterically, the mood shifted and something came over me. There was a brief pause. Before I had time to question it, my secret came pouring from my freshly kissed lips, and I knew I would never be the same.

From the moment I met this man, I felt so safe, and I believe that's why it felt effortless to share the deepest secret of my soul with someone who was still essentially a stranger. With him, I felt seen. I felt heard. I felt supported and held fully. I had never felt this way with a man in my life, and it was then that I realized the power of being in the presence of a man of integrity. It was clear that he respected himself and, in turn, it was intrinsic for him to respect others—even me, the one who felt broken. I longed to be loved unconditionally, but before that could happen, I had to get honest about my shadow and learn to love all of my parts, equally.

Let Your Darkness Illuminate the Light

We all have shadow parts of ourselves. For many, these are unconscious until we are willing to recognize and admit they exist. Oftentimes, when we meet our shadows for the first time, we are overwhelmed with judgment, shame, or a similar emotion. What we fail to recognize, though, is the role these shadows play and how, in reality, they may actually be some of our greatest tools for growth.

So let's talk about the shadow self.

In psychology, the shadow contains all the parts of you that you don't really want to look at or admit to possessing. One way to begin recognizing these pieces is to look at the things that bother you about others, as people can offer mirrors of ourselves. *Where do you notice yourself constantly blaming or judging others? If you look closely, are those characteristics that exist within you?*

An example would be getting annoyed at your partner's laziness when it comes to cleaning up after themself. Or your co-worker who's always late. Or the person with obvious road rage on the highway.

Where do *you* exist in the characteristics you dislike or find yourself judging in others? How can you offer more love and compassion to those areas, accepting them and developing the tools necessary to catch them when they show up and then flip the script in a way that feels more empowering and supportive?

We are born into the world as perfectly imperfect beings. Over time, we begin to form beliefs based on our conditioning, experiences, and societal expectations/programming. Oftentimes, we push down pieces of our true selves. When this happens, our innocence becomes watered down, and we adapt to become a new version of ourselves. I happen to view this *unraveling and becoming* as a beautiful thing, something which occurs over and over again in our lifetime.

Perfection is not just overrated, it's total bullshit (much like Bigfoot, it doesn't exist). We all have our own version of trauma, whether we want to admit it to the world (or ourselves) or not. Healing is not about working toward perfection, it's about accepting our entire being and vowing to love all of ourselves, no matter what or who we become in spite of our circumstances.

Healing is messy and often uncomfortable as fuck! And still, on the other side of healing lies our freedom. I don't know about you, but I happen to think that makes all of the discomfort totally worth it. I recommend getting cozy with your wholeness and accepting that there will be pieces you don't like. Regardless of this, I'm inviting you to make a conscious choice to keep going anyway, as you learn to accept and love all of yourself and adapt what you feel needs work as you step into the life you're creating.

The Only Way Over is Through

I know the idea of pushing the ickiness down—or doing whatever possible to forget that any of it even happened—seems way more appealing than actually facing it, feeling it, and becoming friends with it. But because I love you and I am committed to your transformation, I'm going to give it to you straight.

Doing anything other than facing it, sitting with it, and moving through the discomfort in whatever way you need to ***for you,*** *is not only a waste of precious time and energy but will prevent you from finding the space to fully heal.*

Sure, you might feel better temporarily. But I can say with 100% certainty that the emotions you're working so hard to stuff deep down inside will find their way back into your experience, likely manifesting in things you don't recognize as related at all.

These might look like weight gain, acne, headaches, depression, leaky gut, autoimmune disease, unhealthy relationships, lack of boundaries, addiction, insomnia, self-sabotaging cycles, fatigue.

Should I go on?

It's true that the pain you feel in the process of diving in and doing the work to get on the other side will be hard at times. You will likely have days that feel gross and impossible. It may send you into a spiral of thoughts like, *No fucking way, I can't do this.* But guess what? Those shitty emotions will eventually begin to fade, and seemingly out of nowhere you'll find yourself smiling for no reason, laughing a little harder, and coming home to yourself once again (or maybe for the first time).

And here's the real kicker.

As I write these words to you now, more than two decades post-sexual assault, with years of healing work and tools to support the ongoing journey of healing...I still struggle at times. Because I'm human!

I struggle to love myself in the moments where I don't feel worthy of love. I struggle to accept love from others, afraid at times that if I do their love will leave me. I struggle to embrace my darkness when it rears its head and begs for my attention. I struggle to show up when what I want to do is hide. I struggle to remember my strength when I am feeling weak, lost, uncertain, scared. I struggle to accept that it's all perfect and that every single moment is truly a gift, even when I feel like life is collapsing around me.

I understand wanting the pain to just disappear, and if I had a magic wand and could make that happen for you, I would. But the reality is, **overcoming the struggle is where the lessons lie.** And the sooner you choose to push through the fear and discomfort and see what you're made of, the sooner you'll find yourself on the other side of it all stronger, healthier, happier, and more resilient than you knew possible.

Of course the experience itself won't go away. But I want to encourage you to step into loving even the moments that have caused you pain. Remember, every moment in your life has helped to shape you into the incredibly brave and courageous person you are, even when you don't exactly feel brave or courageous.

It is impossible for a single moment to define you, unless you give it that power.

So don't.

Feel the fear, and show up. Cry your eyeballs out, and show up. Sit on the kitchen floor in your underwear eating spoonfuls of Nutella, and *show the fuck up!*

Showing up can mean many different things, so decide how you can best honor your own definition of "showing up," and commit to being in the practice of that honoring—every single day. As an example, for me showing up means slowing down when I want to speed up as a way to disconnect and hide. Showing up means following through on the commitments I've made even when I don't feel like it (not to be confused with neglecting my body's signals to rest). Showing up means feeling the feelings as a way to move *through* them instead of distracting myself as a way to move *past* them (ignoring). When we choose to show up—for ourselves, first and foremost—we train our mind and body to feel safe in our decision-making ability. We reframe our internal survival state that was created out of necessity (thank you, body), but has since become our default—a low vibrational baseline in our attempt to operate freely and authentically in the world.

The world has so much pain and hatred already. It's our responsibility to choose better so we can show others what's possible when we decide *enough is enough.* We are not victims. The moment you were harmed, your safety and security were taken. But you survived every moment before and every moment since, which in my opinion makes you a goddamn warrior!

What has happened in your life was never meant to break you. And in the next chapter I will dive into what I mean, and share with you how you can begin the process of freeing yourself from the pain so you can embrace all that's available to you.

Why Me?

Inevitably this seems to be one of the first questions we ask ourselves after any sort of trauma. We try to find the reason it happened, questioning what we did wrong, what we could've done differently. We look for a way to blame others or, possibly, for a way to blame ourselves. Part of the frustration of trauma is that no matter why it happened, it happened. And nothing you think, say or do can change that. (I know, ugh!)

If you were able to have all your questions answered, do you think it would be enough? Do you think that if your assailant gave you a reason why they did what they did, it would justify the pain they caused? That you would feel better? That you would be able to forget about it and move on?

No. Because what they did will never be okay. What happened sucks! But you are not bad. You are not broken. You are not wrong. You are not damaged. You are not at fault. You are not cursed. You are not destined for pain. *You were given something hugely challenging to overcome.* And I believe we are all fully capable of healing.

Trauma is not something we ask for, and it's not something I would wish upon anyone. It's also not something that can be justified, excused or explained. Sometimes, we just need to accept things for what they are and find a way to use our experiences to our advantage. I happen to believe trauma is one of those things.

When I talk to people about their healing process, there are many different roads traveled. Totally okay. What works for you may not work for me, and vice versa. But there are a couple key factors that are necessary in order to truly move *through* the experience and be able to heal, instead of suppressing what happened—because when we suppress, we add a whole other layer to the trauma, often expressing itself physically as illness or disease.

Notice I said move *through*? We talk about *getting over* things, but if we skip the stuff causing the emotional response in the first place, we're kind of missing the point of true healing, don't you think? Feeling it all isn't exactly comfortable. But I really do believe it's necessary in order to release it and start again. Re-traumatization is something we want to avoid, so working with someone who can safely guide your process is invaluable.

To begin our journey toward healing, we must first **acknowledge that it happened and accept that it can't be undone.**

I know. It can feel really scary, but it's true. And the sooner you allow yourself to do that, the sooner you will be on your way to freedom.

In her brilliant book, *When Things Fall Apart: Heart Advice for Difficult Times*, Pema Chödrön says, "Rather than letting our negativity get the better of us, we could acknowledge that right now we feel like a piece of shit and not be squeamish about taking a good look. That's the compassionate thing to do. That's the brave thing to do. We could smell that piece of shit. We could feel it; what is its texture, color, and shape? We can explore the nature of that piece of shit. We can know the nature of dislike, shame, and embarrassment and not believe there's something wrong with that."

Essentially, we can be with the shit without letting it consume us.

And then there's the *sitting in the shit* part of healing. This is where you allow yourself to be with the pain, the experience, the emotions, the confusion, the grief, the sorrow, the loss. You grant yourself permission to be human and have the same compassion for yourself as you would a dear friend going through something similar.

The *being with* is the difficult part, and it's easy to get stuck there. But when you think about it from the perspective of literally sitting in shit, ask yourself: *how long am I willing to stay here before I decide that enough is enough?* I think we can all agree that eventually, remaining in the stench (the pain) would become unbearable. At which point you get to decide what the acceptable timeframe for rumination and stagnation looks like *for you.*

So decide.

Do this for yourself. Do it for your future and the life still available to you. Because even though you're different now, and your priorities may have shifted, your dreams are achievable. The life you hoped to create before this happened is still waiting for you to grab onto it. Your burning desire for more is proof that yes, you are capable, and anything is possible.

There is no right or wrong timing for your healing, my dear. Whatever feels true for you is perfect. But before you make that decision, I want to encourage you to get really honest with yourself.

Here are some questions to consider as you work to move through the pain:

1. Is how I feel right now supporting where I want to go?
2. If I were free of (pain, anger, sadness, grief—insert your truest emotions), how would my life improve?
3. How do I want to feel instead?
4. How much longer am I willing to stay here before I decide to move in the direction of my dreams, and choose a better feeling state?

Sitting in your shit, as I call it, is different for everyone and the process of finding your way out is never glamorous. What I love about healing, though, is the person we become in the process...including our shadow parts illuminating the darkness that we all have within, which often find a way to come forward in our most tender of moments.

As I mentioned, it took me three-and-a-half years to speak up. For you, it may be shorter, it may be longer. You may also feel like you'll never share this piece of yourself openly, which again, is entirely up to you. What I will say, though, is that when I finally did share my story for the first time, it was almost as if the decision was not mine, but that of my subconscious as a necessity in order for me to move forward and begin living again. Speaking it aloud worked for me. But that may not be your path. Honor whatever feels true for you. You don't owe anyone an explanation.

I am often asked, *How did you know it was the right time? What was the reaction you got? How did you feel afterward?*

And while I am always happy to share this information, my experience will be different than anyone else's simply because we are all individual beings having our own individual experiences. So while our collective truth begging to be set free may have the same undertone of trauma, the actual event and everything to follow is deeply personal.

I want you to take a moment and close your eyes. Take a few deep breaths in through your nose and out through your mouth. Notice what's coming up for you. Notice where in your body you're feeling the sensations, the emotions, the doubt, or anything else. Be with it, and send love to those places.

When you feel the whirring begin to dissipate, open your eyes.

It's time to get to work.

2

What Was Harming Them?

"The feeling that she had never really lived in this world caught her by surprise. It was a fact. She had never lived. Even as a child, as far back as she could remember, she had done nothing but endure. She had believed in her own inherent goodness, her humanity, and lived accordingly, never causing anyone harm. Her devotion to doing things the right way had been unflagging, all her successes had depended on it, and she would have gone on like that indefinitely. She didn't understand why, but faced with those decaying buildings and straggling grasses, she was nothing but a child who had never lived."
– Han Kang, The Vegetarian

When I think back to being a kid, I remember the freedom and ease I felt knowing that I would be taken care of. I was fortunate, as I've since come to realize that not everyone can say that about their childhood.

I can remember my Nana always saying, "Be kind to everyone, for we never know the battle others are fighting." At the time, I didn't really understand the last part of her statement. I mean, I was thinking about recess and what kind of snacks my mom packed in my lunch. What could a small child have to be upset about?

Turns out, quite a lot, actually. But I wouldn't understand the magnitude of that truth until many years later when I found myself in my own darkness, curious where the anger, pain and sadness came from when I was surrounded by so much love.

My Nana used to say that everyone deserves love, that it is our responsibility to be an example of it for ourselves and the world as a whole. Again, as a kid I was more focused on the simple things, like what kind of jelly to put on the (very burnt) toast my mom had made me for breakfast, or what shirt to wear to school. It wasn't until I got older that the reality of her words sank in.

No matter how hard we try, we never really know what's going on in the lives of others. And I believe this is a big reason why it's imperative that we treat everyone as though we are the only source of love they'll encounter in their day. Maybe even in their lifetime.

What would happen if instead of judging others, we committed to loving them? How different would our world be? I'd like to think it would not only make a massive difference, but that love itself could actually be the anecdote to heal our planet and our collective hearts.

Baby, You Were Born This Way

We are born into this world innocent, completely oblivious to the darkness around us and within us (that pesky shadow side). It is only through our lived experiences—what we're taught by our caregivers, peers and the world, as well as through our lineage (intergenerational trauma)—that we begin to label things and people as good or bad.

Looking back, I'm pretty sure my Nana and my mom loved me extra hard in hopes that the darkness they'd encountered and still held onto, as well as what I encountered at a young age, would be forgotten. Or at the very least, diminished. On one hand, these two incredible women slayed the game when it came to loving me hard, fiercely, and unconditionally. But there's something to be said for our intelligent bodies, too. And the fact that no matter how much love you pour into a person, unless they've taken the time to heal the root of the pain, it will find a way to resurface.

For me, my life began in a single-parent home. My mom had just turned 22 years old when I was born, and although she'd prayed for a blonde-haired, blue-eyed little girl all her life, the timing of my arrival wasn't exactly planned or convenient. I'm also pretty sure she didn't envision raising a strong-willed, outspoken, opinionated child on her own, either. But as Woody Allen put it, "If you want to make God laugh, tell him about your plans." Adaptability is a must, no matter what stage of life you're in and thankfully, my mom had this trait dialed in.

I only have one memory of my biological father. I was about two years old, twirling around in my favorite yellow dress. He was in the kitchen making me a grilled cheese sandwich.

As he called for me to come and get it, I began running in circles through the living room and kitchen (my mom and I lived in a small two-bedroom apartment) squealing with joy, "You have to catch me first!" Of course, that's my recollection. Whether or not it's totally accurate, I have no idea, but I've held onto that memory all my life because I remember feeling so carefree and happy. I felt safe. And for that small moment in time, my heart felt loved by my father.

Other than that single memory, I would never get the chance to know the man who helped bring me into this world. My father was an addict, whose thirst had him reaching for booze and other substances instead of protecting me as my father and friend. Maybe I felt like a burden to him, or maybe he was just ashamed of his inability to support us due to his love for the bottle. Either way, my mom never spoke ill of him. In fact, she had nothing but lovely things to say about him...when he was sober, anyway.

As a kid, I didn't know any different. But as an adult, my desire for answers grew. I wanted to know why he left. Had I done something wrong? What I later found out was that my mom had asked him to leave while I was still just the size of some sorta fruit in her womb, after he'd come home wasted, yet again. It was in the midst of an argument when my father kicked her in her swollen, pregnant belly that she drew a line in the sand. She refused to endure his abuse any longer and made the courageous decision to find a way to support the life growing inside of her, as well as her own.

From that moment forward, my mom would stand as my greatest protector and best friend. My father had his own demons to conquer, as many of us do. But not once did my mom say anything negative about him, despite the pain he caused during the course of their relationship. Whenever I would ask about him, she would tell me how funny he was, how he was always the life of the party. Apparently, he was also a great chef as well as a pool shark that owned the table everywhere he played. I didn't find out about his darkness until I was much older, and even then my mom shared her experience and what she knew of his past with a sense of stoicism, free of judgment. She embodied absolute compassion, which I believe she did for her own survival along with the protection of my heart. My mother, while not perfect, is an angel. I am so glad that I chose to be her daughter in this lifetime and that, despite all the chaos, she chose to bring me into the world.

Revisiting My Abandonment Wounds

When I was 20, nearly a year after I'd been raped, I got a call from my father. It was the first time in my life I can remember speaking to him. He called to apologize for his absence, asking about my life, curious as to the woman I'd become. We chatted briefly before there was a long pause on the other end of the line, which was eventually filled by his humble request for forgiveness. He let me know that he would understand if I couldn't forgive him, he'd really "messed up," and I could hear the trepidation in his breath as a thunderous silence stood between us.

The truth was, I couldn't recall ever being angry at him, only confused and hurt as to why he'd never been around. I assured him that I'd had a really beautiful life, despite the void of a consistent father figure. I'd spent my entire life without him present, so being without him was all I knew. Forgiveness, at least in the way I interpreted it, felt easy in this sense. I'd accepted long before our phone call that his addiction had nothing to do with me, and I had no doubt that he must have been in a lot of pain to have chosen such a lonely, toxic lifestyle instead of getting clean and experiencing parenthood and all that came with it. I guess it might've been lucky for him though, as I was not the easiest child to raise. (Sorry, mom!)

Once the silence ran its course, he cleared his throat before mustering the courage to share the real reason for his call, so many years after he'd disappeared from my life.

He told me that he was getting his affairs in order because, as fate would have it, he was dying. Stage 4 colon cancer. He wanted me to know that he'd gotten updates on my life over the years from his sister (my aunt, whom I'd kept in touch with), and that he was proud of me. I'll always remember those words. I asked if I could meet him in person, hoping there would be enough time to do so before he passed, a request he seemed surprised by, but one he welcomed. We spent the next 30 minutes or so discussing my plans to visit him where he'd been living for years, in Florida, in the coming months. Little did I know, though, we'd only get one more phone call before his time was up.

It was only a few weeks later that the phone rang, and I heard the nervous compassion in my mom's voice on the other end. She was calm, but I could tell something was off. She has always had a way of remaining level headed during life's hardest moments, and this was no different.

"Honey, I need to share something with you…are you sitting down?" She continued, "Your father…he passed away last night. He's at peace now. I'm so sorry." I didn't hear anything that followed.

My father died on October 15, 2001, exactly a year to the day of my assault just a year prior, something I didn't realize until sifting through old paperwork years later.

The news rocked my world more than I could've imagined. I knew the shock was coming, but it happened so fast! I was flooded with deep sadness, followed by an overwhelming sense of anger and resentment. *How dare you! Why are you always leaving me? Fuck you for dying!*

Once again, I felt abandoned by the man who was supposed to love and protect me...the man who chose booze and drugs over being my dad. While it confused the hell out of me at the time, and as hard as it was to admit, I now know it was never personal. His actions had nothing to do with me.

You see, like so many others masking their pain, my father's darkness kept him from being the parent I craved. His addiction consumed him, leaving me and two other children (all from different women) behind to wonder who he was. *Did I look like him? Did we share any similarities? Would we have gotten along? Would he have been a good dad, if he were sober? Where did his demons come from? Did he love me?*

The story of my half-siblings is for another time, but when he passed, let's just say things continued to unfold. Like when, ten years after his death, I got a call from an 18-year-old girl claiming to be my sister. And then a few years later, I got a call from my uncle claiming I had a brother, followed by an email from a 20-something young man claiming to be that said brother (all confirmed through

DNA). I went from growing up primarily as an only child to being the oldest of three in adulthood. And as he was with me, he'd been an absent figure for them as well. At least he was consistent, I'll give him that.

My father would serve as the first example of abandonment in the story I would later create about men in my life. I wasn't born believing I needed to earn love, none of us are. But over time, I began to question whether or not I was worthy of it. Due to a series of events involving men I'd believed I should've been able to trust, I built a wall around my heart to block the love I yearned for out of fear that it would inevitably be taken away.

My story that *men take what they want and then leave me* felt real. And while a part of me knew that was not true, it would take years for me to finally accept that I had created this belief based on my experiences, but also out of necessity—to make sense of confusion and my own fears as a way to self-protect and find any semblance of internal safety I could.

Hurt People, Hurt People

If you're reading this book, there's a pretty good chance you've been through your own kind of trauma, or you know of someone close to you who has. People often think of trauma as assault or abuse, which are forms of it, sure. But as I've mentioned, trauma wears many masks, comes in many forms, and it certainly doesn't discriminate.

Despite all the pain we're surrounded by, there's a lot of beauty, too. As such, I've chosen to believe that people are not born bad. At least not entirely. I know there are people in this world who are imbalanced and in need of professional help. There are people who are a danger to society, who should not be allowed into the world unsupervised. And I understand there is a whole world out there where horribly indecent people exist, among other unfortunate things. But if you'll notice my wording...*I've* ***chosen*** *to believe that people are not born bad.* As an empath—someone that feels deeply, often absorbing the emotions of others if we're not conscious of our own feelings and state—I find the idea that anyone could intentionally hurt another person "just because" incredibly unsettling. And honestly, sitting in the energy of pain isn't going to help me (or you) create a vibrational match for the life we desire where we are free to be ourselves, surrounded by love and acceptance.

Somewhere along the way, many of us were hurt by someone/something. In turn, our massively intelligent bodies created a cloak of protection as a way to keep us safe. Nobody *wants* to feel pain, so instead, we choose (often subconsciously) to put up walls (which are different from boundaries) hoping we won't feel that shitty feeling anymore. It usually works for a while, but it's not sustainable. And if you're like the majority of people on the planet, then you can't help but crave the basic fundamental human desires for safety, connection, significance, and love. Walls don't allow those needs to be met. Boundaries do.

When you choose walls instead of boundaries, you close yourself off to what's possible on the other side of your old stories and protection patterns. Because walls keep people out. We're talking barbed wire and steel doors.

Think of boundaries as the good ol' South of self-protection. White picket fences, friendly neighbors. Everyone knows each other and looks out for one another. But also, if need be, you can simply lock your door to keep out what doesn't serve you in order to remain, you guessed it, *safe.*

Walls can look like dissociation, where the mind disconnects from thoughts, feelings, memories, even our sense of identity. This often happens subconsciously when a person has experienced a traumatic event or PTSD and disconnects as a way to cope with the pain or feelings surrounded by a lack of safety. When left untreated, this can create bigger problems—avoidant behavior being one of the ways this mental disconnection from Self expresses. Dissociation in the moment, as the traumatic event occurs, is common. This is typically used by our innate intelligence as a way to regulate the nervous system. But it's important to identify this pattern so we can heal it. Otherwise, dissociation has the potential to become a toxic and destructive habit.

As you can see, there's more freedom in boundaries. Boundaries say: *I'm open, and I respect myself enough to say "no" when there's a misalignment. I'm open, and I'm committed to choosing myself first because I love myself that much.*

Where are you putting up walls instead of boundaries in your life? And are you willing to release the barbed wire and replace it with freedom, learning to trust yourself to make decisions from love instead of fear in the process?

Choosing Forgiveness

As I mentioned regarding my experience of being raped, choosing to forgive was never about my assailant, it was about me. The same rings true with the experience with my father.

When we choose to forgive someone, we are not saying that what they did was right or okay. We are consciously *choosing out of* the pain their actions caused and *choosing into* a better feeling state that supports where we want to go. Essentially, we are opting into the freedom forgiveness brings.

Some people believe that you can heal without forgiveness, and maybe that's true. Though I can't help but wonder what might be possible if we allowed ourselves to clear the space being taken up by the hurt and the stored emotions and memories of the experience in our bodies, and instead chose to open up to experiencing better feelings in place of the pain. Because if we don't release our negative emotions, they have to go somewhere. It's like the trunk of a car. If you just kept putting your groceries inside week after week, never taking them into the kitchen, not only would it begin to smell horrible, but eventually there would be no more room for anything else.

The more junk we hold onto that doesn't support the highest version of ourselves, the less space we have to invite the very things we desire to bring into our lives. Forgiveness is just another way of letting go and making room for *more* of all the good that life has to offer us. Otherwise, when every nook and cranny is packed with all the shit we've been through (and will go through), the darkness takes over, blocking the gifts the Universe wants to bless us with.

You may never know why your experience of trauma happened. And I understand the frustration that comes with not knowing, believe me! But ask yourself if the stuckness you're choosing is worth the expansion you're blocking. And if not, then what are you willing to release to feel the emotions you desire as you create a new story?

The reality is, you will likely never get an answer for why it happened. And even if you did get an answer, chances are high that it wouldn't be good enough anyway. Shitty experiences are shitty, and there is no answer in the world that would make the experience less painful. So why waste the energy waiting for something that may never come?

Freedom is your birthright. Your past does not have to define you, nor does your pain. But in order to step into the life waiting for you on the other side of it all, you've got to be willing to choose yourself above all else.

What Was Harming Them?

For those of you lucky enough to get the entire history of your perpetrator's past—being able to understand how they came to be who they are, and why they thought it was reasonable to project their pain onto another human being—huge kudos to you! I hope it helped!

But for the majority of us on the sidelines, waiting for the answers we will never receive, let this be a loving reminder that the answers are not necessary for you to heal and find freedom.

People make mistakes. People make really shitty decisions. People react in confusing ways. People are human...and humans are imperfect.

I'm willing to bet whoever hurt you was hurting in ways you'll never know. I'm also willing to bet that unless they've done some serious work on themselves since the moment they took pieces of you without your permission, and attempted to break you, they're still hurting. Your pain is irrelevant to them. Your suffering means absolutely nothing to them. Your anger does not affect them one bit.

So why are you choosing to keep it?

This is not a moment of judgment but an honest question that I would encourage you to sit with for a time, no matter how uncomfortable. When chatting with fellow survivors at events where I've spoken or online, I've gotten the following answers:

"Holding onto the pain reminds me that it was real, and that I'm not crazy."

"Being angry makes me feel powerful, like I'm somehow in control."

"Forgiveness makes me feel weak, as though I'm saying that what they did was okay."

The list goes on...

None of these responses are wrong. I understand each of these statements. And still I ask: How is any of that supporting the present moment and the future you want to create?

Even if you knew why they did what they did, the event would still be part of your life. And even if they begged and pleaded with you to forgive them, the truth would still remain: somebody hurt you, and you cannot change that. The event has shaped you into the person you are today. The fact that you are still here screams, "I am stronger than my experience, and so I rise. DO YOU HEAR ME? And still, I fucking RISE!"

Yes you do, warrior. Yes. You. Do.

They tried to take your power once, but it's time for you to take that power back and choose yourself—for no other reason than *you are worthy and enough as you are*. You are deserving of internal peace, incredible amounts of joy, and a feeling of true safety in your body as you navigate this crazy world.

Let yourself have it. Let yourself experience the fullness of life as you choose yourself today, and all the days to follow, by allowing yourself to let go and come into a space of acceptance and possibly, forgiveness. Because we have this one life. And how we choose to experience it is ours for the taking.

What does forgiveness mean to you? How do you stretch toward forgiveness instead of away from love? What would it look like, feel like, to be free of the pain you're still holding onto? What is your freedom worth?

3

Who Am I Now?

"Inquire within, rather than without, asking:
'What part of my Self do I wish to experience now?
What aspects of being do I choose to call forth?'
For all of life exists as a tool of your own creation,
and all of its events merely present themselves as opportunities
for you to decide, and be, Who You Are."
– Neale Donald Walsch

Whether we want to admit it or not, we are different on the other side of trauma. Contrary to what we may think, we're not bad, dirty, or damaged. Still, we aren't the same person we were before the trauma occurred. I happen to believe that the *becoming* of our new selves can be one of the most profound (and beautiful) experiences of our lifetimes, if we allow ourselves to be a conscious witness and participant in the unfolding of our new identity, embracing what's available in the process of our radical transformation.

As you can see, I've been through some shit in my life, just as you likely have. And possibly also like you, I've had moments where I felt defeated, pissed off, ready to throw in the towel, and left in a puddle of tears begging for God (or anyone, for that matter) to make the pain stop.

But...*what if the pain was exactly what you needed to become the version of you that's reading this book right now?* What if the pain that left you feeling helpless, weak and confused was actually the very thing necessary to show you the power you hold, and have always held, within?

Trauma often leaves us feeling broken. And maybe we are, at least temporarily. But *broken* can be beautiful (listen to Kelly Clarkson's song, *Broken & Beautiful* for some inspiration), and pain can be healed. Nothing about being human is linear, and in my experience the more we try to force ourselves into a box of impossible standards only to prove we're enough, worthy, and polished to the outside world, the more we lose the core essence of who we are—the versions that existed before and after the wounding occurred.

Our Secrets Keep Us Sick

It wasn't until March of 2004 that I finally broke my silence. It had been three-and-a-half years since the night of my assault, and I couldn't hold onto my secret any longer. I had spent so much time hiding my pain, masking it by staying busy and neglecting myself in the process of proving that I could handle whatever was thrown my way, all on my own. It had become too much—and like water rushing a dam, I couldn't hold the flood of emotions any longer.

While I am grateful to have been brought up by such strong women, the beliefs that were instilled in me, like not relying on anyone (the "you can do it all on your own" mentality) and seeing fierce independence as a badge of honor (which can also be incredibly damaging) didn't help me work through my trauma. In fact, it would take me well into my thirties to realize the power of receiving, and what it meant to allow myself to be truly cared for by anyone.

My secret haunted me. It kept me up at night, counting the hours for the sun to rise and shine a light on my pain. The images from that night penetrated my dreams. Nightmares, really. And all those years later, it still felt surreal.

I had accepted that it had happened, and that my experience of rape was now part of my story. But I had failed to accept the healing process in its entirety to repair my inner world which had been so violently uprooted in a matter of minutes on that cold, rainy October evening.

I just wanted to be normal. I wanted everything around me to be normal. I wanted to pretend like it never happened so I could continue living my life, on my terms, without having to face the reality of it all, which was that I had experienced massive trauma...and I was not okay.

A part of me wishes I could say that my journey was straight forward, that I *finally got through it* without any further complications—and that, eventually, things fell into place. But that would be a big fat lie.

Instead, about six months after my assault, I woke up writhing in pain. It became apparent immediately that not only would I not be making it to my job that afternoon, but there was something seriously wrong happening in my body.

As I looked down at my wrist, I saw a huge, half-baseball sized bump. And I panicked. It was hot to the touch, red, and immobile. Did I sleep on it wrong? Was I having an allergic reaction? At the time, I didn't have insurance, which meant yet another hefty bill to be paid. (You know that whole ectopic pregnancy ordeal? I was billed close to $30k for treatment, which I was able to get assistance with after sending a letter to the hospital's billing department every week for an entire year asking for help. Yes, there is always a solution. Be willing to find it.)

I drove myself to the doctor's office where he scanned my body and wrist, opting not to run any labs given my lack of insurance. Instead, he gave me the diagnosis of rheumatoid arthritis. This made no sense to me. I was 20 years old, in college, modeling at trade shows on the weekends for a local skate and surf brand in Huntington Beach, CA to make ends meet. I was an active student on the Dean's List, with a full social calendar. Debilitating physical pain that left me immobile was not part of the plan.

I left the doctor's office sobbing and called my mom for support. I felt like everything was falling apart—and because I was still holding on so tightly to my secret, there was no room for this new pain to go. The stress of it all felt enormous, and it was showing up physically now.

My twenties were a bit of a blur. What I now understand about trauma is that the blocks in my memory surrounding my rape are common, even normal (more on that in Chapter 6). I'm not sure I will ever recover them, but I find it comforting to know that new memories are always available and that maybe, it's better that some things have been left in the past.

That doctor's visit was the just beginning of what would become a nine year struggle for my survival. While my friends spent their college years and subsequent twenties out and about, partying their way through life without a care in the world, my experiences were much different.

The physical pain only grew worse, and I found myself spiraling into a depression that felt all consuming. My body wasn't working, and it frustrated the hell out of me! I would wake up most mornings with red, swollen, tender joints, unable to crawl out of bed let alone walk to the bathroom and shower. Things got so bad, I had to have friends come over and help me with everything, including washing my hair and getting dressed afterward. I had always been fiercely independent, even as a young girl. Asking for help felt incredibly uncomfortable and vulnerable.

I'd lived an active lifestyle, playing sports growing up, cheerleading throughout high school, even attempting to pick up soccer again when I moved to San Diego (which was hilarious because even though I'd played on a select team as a teenager, I was absolutely awful as an adult). I worked out, ate fairly healthy (although imbalanced, in retrospect), practiced mindfulness and yoga. By all accounts, I was living and breathing the gold standard of a healthy lifestyle. Yet here I was, sick and without answers, unable to do the simplest tasks on my own.

My memory was foggy at best, my sleep erratic, my energy at rock bottom. I was a total mess both emotionally and physically. And somehow, I managed to graduate college with honors. Sure, I was stubborn. But my incessant need to succeed against all odds was a bandaid for my pain that had become unhealthy, and it was screaming at me to pay attention.

The pain persisted, as did the setbacks. Every doctor I saw gave me a different diagnosis, all of them prescribing me a myriad of drugs to help with the pain (otherwise known as "symptom management"). Aside from the problem of putting bandaids on the real underlying issue—which nobody addressed, or seemed to understand—I was allergic to nearly everything I was given, inevitably sending me to the hospital with a fever, rash, or whatever else my fighting body could muster as a way to reject the potential "solution."

I spent many nights, even weeks, in the hospital—for *nine whole years*. I was diagnosed with everything...from meningitis, to ruptured ovarian cysts, to "mystery" illnesses, even a kidney infection so bad that the nurse called my mom two states away to let her know she should come—they weren't sure I would make it. That visit alone left me drugged up in a hospital bed for over a week, reading crappy celebrity gossip magazines and dreaming of my old life where I felt whole and capable. Unstoppable, even.

Secrets. Fuck, man. They really do limit us. It's like the moment I opened my mouth and shared about being raped, my body took its first breath only to release every toxic person, thought, food, you name it, that I had ever inhaled or experienced. And then my body stirred them all up to be thrown out all at once. Except my petite and fragile body, not to mention my nervous system, didn't have the capacity to hold the weight of the load. Instead, my body crumbled under the pressure of past pain and silent trauma.

All in all, it took nine specialists to finally confirm what my mom had suspected all along, and I finally reluctantly accepted. After trying every medication they knew to try, including weekly injections that didn't seem to do much other than piss me off, my "illness" now had a name: Systemic Lupus Erythematosus (SLE). Paired with Sjogren's Syndrome, Raynaud's Phenomenon, and (years later) Hashimoto's Thyroiditis.

There was a sense of relief in knowing that I wasn't coo-coo-bananas—followed by anger and determination. *Why did it take so long to properly diagnose me? And fuck off if you think I am taking one more god-damned pill or injection ever again!* Let's just say, I didn't have the best opinion of Western medicine after that.

It was during the worst years of my illnesses that I became my own guinea pig. What did I have to lose? I began reading incessantly. I studied Western medicine, Eastern medicine, plant medicine, shamanism, essential oils, herbs, every diet I could find. Whatever I could get my hands on, I tried. I started looking at food for what it was—the real medicine. I dove into mindset work, and I revisited the philosophy that my Nana had always worked so hard to instill in me: *we are in control of our thoughts which create our actions and, thus, our reality.* All of this knowledge and research blew me wide open.

And just like that, everything made so much sense. Armed with the newfound understanding of the body, I knew I would never be the same. After a decade of self-study under my belt, I made the decision to go back to school and study Holistic Health and Nutrition. My focus had always been around autoimmune disease, but I knew I'd only scratched the surface. I was hungry for more. I not only wanted to find a natural solution to heal my own body, since clearly nothing else was working. But I also wanted to learn as much as I could so that I could share my knowledge with others. I thought that if I could help even one person avoid all the pain and frustration I'd been through, all of my years of struggling to find answers would be worth it.

I was right.

Mourning the Old Self

Looking back, it's hard to believe I endured the path I had walked for so long. I don't recognize the old "victim" version of me that I see in pictures, with swollen cheeks from 18 months on prednisone and tired eyes that hadn't slept in weeks. I looked empty, lost, even sad. And despite my attempts at holding it all together as best I could, those who knew me best knew better.

I remember the *me* before it happened...spirited, adventurous, and blessed with more energy than I could expend. But she was gone, and in her place I was left with a stranger that had taken up residence in my broken down body. This new, incredibly raw version of myself was hidden somewhere within, and like any new friend, it would take time to get to know her, trust her, and love her fully. I just kept reminding myself, *I am alive.* It was okay that I was a bit more guarded, that made sense given what I'd been through. But I *wanted* to let my walls down. I *wanted* to feel safe to be held and let love in. As I continued to lean in and do my best to get to know the new me, I remained committed to embracing my becoming and finding the lessons within my experience—which, although not necessary for everyone, felt important to me.

I've always had a hard time letting go of things and people my soul has grown fond of. I'm not sure if it's due to my sensitive constitution and watery heart, or simply the fact that I made a promise to the Universe long ago that I would do my best to never allow anyone to feel abandoned by me, the way I had felt so many times in my life.

Either way, letting go of my identity to become the young woman I was growing into felt absolutely terrifying. It felt as though I was literally pulling my limbs from my body with pliers, while praying they'd grow back, somehow stronger than before. I felt the physical *tearing* on such a deep, visceral level that I wasn't sure it would be possible to put the strewn-out pieces of myself back together again. I was a real life Humpty Dumpty.

When I finally spoke my truth, through apprehensive lips, I felt as though I was having an out of body experience. I had masked my pain and shock in charisma, which matched the old version of me. But that outward confidence didn't match how I really felt inside. I felt hollow and completely out of my element. I asked myself...

Who are you?
Why are you still here?
What will you do with this experience?
When will you realize you are still loveable, valuable, worthy, and enough?

On one hand, I'd spent years consciously choosing to remain silent. And on another, I didn't feel like I'd had a choice. I had acceptance nailed down—and I'd gotten really good at forgiveness, but I had yet to come to terms with the repercussions of my experience. I had yet to come to terms with what it meant to reinvent myself in a way that still matched the dreams I had *and* the vision of myself I'd been working so hard to realize.

Saying goodbye to the 19-year-old me who'd existed before my innocence was stolen became life altering. And it took time. I actually don't think I allowed myself to fully let go until the moment I chose to open my mouth and share my truth for the first time. And even then, there remained a lot of unpacking to do.

I'd made a home in the body of the girl who'd walked into that house on that particular rainy October night. And I didn't want to leave her there, alone and afraid, either. So as we do with those we love, I took her with me. And remnants of her stayed with me for many years after.

Truthfully, there will likely always be pieces of her innocence within me, tucked into old memories, as the creator of some of my wildest dreams. I loved her, but looking back I can see that I didn't value her, not the way she deserved. Facing my experience of trauma served as a second chance to start over, to learn what it really meant to love, honor, respect, and value myself from a place of enoughness, no longer trying to prove myself to earn my keep.

Shifting Our Identity

Whether you're a survivor or not, chances are good that you aren't the same person you were even a year ago. While I have no doubt that the prior version of you was amazing, you've likely outgrown that particular version and moved into someone wiser (and older, but who's counting).

This is your invitation to say goodbye, to let the past go.

To those who don't know your past, the truth of all that you've experienced may be too much to hold. The thought of getting to the root of the person you used to be in order to become the brilliance you are now may feel irrelevant… or seemingly unnecessary for others to even try to comprehend. None of which matters, however, because either way, you're incredible. You always have been.

And, in spite of it all, the truth remains: no matter who you were, who you are now, or who you will inevitably become… you will always be too much for somebody, trauma or not.

Different. The same. Constantly evolving. Learning. Growing. Fucking up. Making amends. Doing the best you can. You are still here, glorious and purposeful. ALIVE.

Where you've been, along with the space you're stepping into, it's enough. You're enough. All that you're becoming is more than enough. Every single confusing piece of the starry constellation that *is you* has been created with fierce intention and care. Thank you for being brave with your pain and your life.

Your past brought you here, this is true. But your past is not who you are today. Only you can create purpose from the multitude of lessons available from each experience, should you choose to press forward and give these lessons meaning.

Don't push your painful moments away as if they're nothing—you survived! And don't judge yourself or others for past choices. What matters is the *you* who has risen. You can choose to show up fully each day, raw in your humanness, real in your watery imperfections and wilted rose petal fields of a journey well traveled.

You're not broken. You're not damaged. You're a masterpiece. Art. How people choose to see you is their perception. However, perception is only a sliver of the truth.

Your scars, your tears, your misspoken words...they were all necessary to assemble the intricate puzzle that has become *you* in this moment.

Brave. Bold. Beautiful.

A genius at being human, I bow to you. To your strength and your struggle. To your dedication to the progression of realizing and fully living in the truth that resides within the newest version of you.

You are enough.
More than.
You are all of it wrapped into one perfectly imperfect form.

Who Am I Now?

Based on your experiences, you've been asked to form new agreements with the Universe to match the frequency of your current reality. Speaking in esoteric terms, agreements are simply things that have been decided *with* and *by* us before we physically came into this human experience. In the spiritual sense, you can think of agreements as contracts between you and God, Universe, Spirit—who or whatever you resonate with. These contracts are soul connections with the important and impactful people in our lives who help us learn what we came here to learn in order to grow into more self-aware and spiritually connected beings.

Circumstances have changed you, and now you have lived experiences that have shifted the way you move through life, understandably. Because of this, it may be time to recalibrate to this new version of yourself by sitting down and getting honest about who you are now, how you are evolving, what you need, desire, and dream of becoming. Have a conversation with yourself—invite in a higher power should you feel called to do so. Whatever you need to feel aligned with the path you're walking now, as the person you are now, do that.

Allow yourself to find freedom in the releasing of the old as you call in the new. There's magic there. Just remember, your traumas don't define you. They're simply *part of* you.

We tend to find solace in labels. I think this is because somewhere within "acceptable" labels lies a glimpse of our soul that connects us to our desires, whether pure or ego-driven. We then attach to those labels, hoping they will fill the void of the work we still have left to do. Instead, they tend to water down our truth and leave us grasping for more of what we believe will allow others to see us in a particular way, neglecting the importance of choosing ourselves, as we are.

As we shift, so do our thoughts, beliefs, and actions. Trauma has a way of speeding up the process or, at times, slowing it down as we take the time to breathe and find our new path. Either way, I think the biggest challenge with change stemming from trauma is that we were not given a choice. Maybe we wanted to stay the same...and not being able to go back can feel unfair. This inability can create a multitude of emotions that seem hard to understand, let alone navigate and deal with.

But one thing I know for sure is that even the most horrendous acts—based on our individual perception of the event—have a purpose.

We might not grasp or make sense of these things in the moment or even years later. And we sure as hell might feel like we got the short end of the stick at times. But our beliefs about our experiences are ours. That means, **we choose**. That's how we take back our power.

Who I was before I was raped is not the same person who stood up and walked herself back to her car. She is not the same person who graduated college with honors. She is not the same person who started her own business. And she is not the same person who continues to love deeply, no matter the cost.

The person you used to be before you were hurt is gone. Who you choose to continue becoming on your journey will change as you learn new skills, develop new insights, and gain a deeper understanding of your wants and needs.

Trauma or not, we change. That's part of the human experience.

If we participate in the practice of growth (something I highly recommend), we must become really good at releasing, *mourning* if we must, the person we were in the past—whether she existed five minutes or five years ago.

I promise you, the pieces you loved about your old self still remain. They've just taken a different form. This next version of you becomes an invitation to step into newness, to be open to what's available. Allow yourself to let go and receive the gifts making their way to you now.

Something that really supported me in my healing that may support you, too, is writing a letter to the version of you that existed before you were hurt.

What do you want the past *you* to know?
What are you holding onto that needs to be released?

Tell her. Remind her she's safe to emote, express, and experience all that life has in store from this moment forward.

This is your invitation to start over, and believe that the best is yet to come.

Because who you are is whoever you decide to be. So be free. Be wild. Be authentically and unapologetically *you!* And trust that it's enough...because you are enough...you always will be.

4

Is It Possible to Love My Broken Parts?

"Having compassion starts and ends with having compassion for all those unwanted parts of ourselves, all those imperfections that we don't even want to look at. Compassion isn't some kind of self-improvement project or ideal that we're trying to live up to."
– Pema Chödrön, When Things Fall Apart

After the rape, everything I had known about myself now felt like a distant memory, or possibly like it had never existed in the first place—I wasn't sure. What was left was a puzzle strewn about—some pieces missing, other pieces searching for their counterparts to become whole. Looking in the mirror felt like I was staring at shattered glass—nothing seemed to make any sense and yet, somehow it was still beautiful. When I close my eyes now and think of that tender, seemingly fragile version of myself, I can see so clearly how the experience of being raped shaped me into the woman I am now. It's through this new lens that I can look back with compassion at the shattered memory of sorts, and appreciate the courage it took to keep showing up and love myself back to wholeness.

Trauma does that. It lends itself to the confusion of, "What's left?"—and begs us to ponder the question, *"Now what?"* I, too, used to call myself broken. But the truth is, I wasn't. And neither are you.

There's a beautiful story about the centuries-old Japanese art of fixing broken pottery called *Kintsugi.* When the pottery cracks or breaks, instead of using something to hide the imperfections, they use a tree sap dusted with gold, silver, or platinum. Once the pottery has been put back together in this way, it leaves beautiful, golden seams throughout the piece giving it its own unique blueprint. Instead of hiding the fractures, they're illuminated as a way to celebrate the journey and what's been overcome. In the end, these pieces are seen as even more beautiful, and given a second chance.

Survivorship reminds me of this ancient art form, reminding us to see our internal scars (trauma) as the golden thread that has allowed us to put ourselves back together, and begin again. We may have been through something terrible, but the fact remains that ***we are still here.*** Which means we got a second chance where so many others don't, and that's pretty incredible.

Returning to Wholeness

Through the pain of perceived brokenness, as survivors we often take on the story that we'll never be whole. This is commonly followed by the very real fear of something like, *Who will love me this way?*

And as big as this realization feels—that you are different now and you have no idea what that actually means—equally important is the work necessary to release the remnants of the old you, to make room for the next version of you, a sort of stranger in your own skin. Wholeness doesn't come from our experiences, or the opinions of others. Wholeness happens when we learn to love and accept all of our pieces, light and dark alike. In order to do this, we must be brave enough to accept what's happened, and find a way to live with our new reality, embracing our *becoming* every step of the way. This does not mean the anger, shame, guilt, blame, or whatever emotions come up go away overnight. But it can mean that we commit to our personal evolution because we realize (and accept) that we're someone worthy of loving deeply, being loved fully, and belonging.

From this awareness of self, we open to life and find that we have all we need within. As humans, shifting and transformation is normal, trauma or not. It looks different for everybody, and that doesn't make it right or wrong, it makes it real.

Let your experiences open you. Wholeness is your birthright, not something earned or accomplished. *They* did not break you, my dear. But they did open you up to the unknown—a scary reality for us all in some capacity. Just as you do when meeting someone new, get curious. Ask questions. Listen. And as you align with the truth that arises, lean deeper into love, trusting that the "holes" created by your trauma were merely catalysts, allowing you to step further into yourself, and the person you will inevitably become because of it.

To be whole is to *be*...to exist. There is no reason to run from your pieces, for they have all been carefully and beautifully crafted to assemble the masterpiece that is the one and only *you*. In fact, we need the duality between our wholeness (light) and our perceived scattered pieces (shadow self, or darkness) for without each, neither would be possible. I'll explain why each is important below.

Dismantling Beliefs

Maybe your parts have loosened a bit. Or maybe you feel as though you've come completely undone. That's okay. Either way, you're not broken. You can't be. You've been given an experience which has provided you the opportunity to transform...to expand...to grow and evolve because of it. So open your arms, open your heart, and shift toward the light like a flower seeking warmth. Allow yourself to wiggle and sway with the discomfort and uncertainty as you welcome a new beginning.

This is the path you were destined for, even if it doesn't make a lick of sense to you right now. You may not have chosen it, but it chose you. So what will you do with it?

The more conversations I have with fellow survivors, the more it becomes abundantly clear that one of the most challenging things about all of this unraveling is figuring out how to reframe our thoughts in a way that supports our current reality in a positive way. When we are in the shit, it's hard to see anything outside of it. But the goal is to move forward, to not remain stuck. And in order for that to happen, we need to stretch ourselves into the practice of cultivating a more empowering internal dialogue, which means choosing better feeling thoughts that align with our desired state.

Just as we water a garden, we must water the seeds of our mind. Consciously choosing what we feed our mind becomes imperative on the path toward healing and, ultimately, our freedom. It's often easier said than done, but the more we lean into the discomfort as we create a new habit, the easier the positive habit becomes over time.

As a book writing coach, I use the following exercise with my writing students—because it works! Possibly like you, many of my students are also survivors in one way or another, so they relate to the inner turmoil that often accompanies trauma and how it affects our day-to-day lives.

So let's talk about patterns.

When it comes to patterns, old habits die hard, which can be annoying but also makes sense. Patterns are familiar. They're comfortable. They're also taking up precious space where better feeling thoughts could be hanging out and helping to support the life you're working so hard to create.

Our subconscious mind (which controls roughly 90% of our thoughts and actions) is a tricky little thing! In order to reframe, and ultimately rewire our beliefs and thought patterns, we've gotta get honest with ourselves about where we're holding ourselves back in the first place, including the root of the beliefs we've deemed to be true.

I know it may be hard to hear, but *you* are usually the thing in the way. And the blockage begins with your beautiful, brilliant mind.

I want you to ask yourself the following questions without shame, blame, guilt or judgment. This is not about being a victim, this is about creating awareness so you can create something better moving forward. Take 20 minutes or so and go through this exercise. You may be surprised as to what comes up.

Here are some prompts to move you into your truth so you can shift as needed...

What stories are you still holding onto from your past that are keeping you stuck today? *Examples could be: I'm not smart enough; I will never make a ton of money; Money is for assholes, and I'm not an asshole; Nobody wants to hear what I have to say; I'm not worthy of abundance or having an amazing life; I'm unlovable...everybody leaves me.*

Where do these beliefs come from? *This is a massive awareness point that often feels really scary to dive into and admit. Totally okay. Be with whatever comes up. It could be something or someone in your childhood; it could be from a past experience. Dig deep and find the dirt!*

How are these beliefs holding you back? *Examples: Because of this belief, I don't trust people...I keep my guard up...My body is breaking down...I'm broke and unhappy...I'm single...*

Now for the fun part—the reframe! This is where you get to reprogram your subconscious and tell it a new, more empowering story, one that feels supportive and most importantly...true!

You'll probably slip up along the way because, you know, this whole *human* thing. Give yourself a break, though. Those thoughts taking up space in your head won't just change overnight. I mean, think of all the years it's taken to nail down the beliefs you have right now!

The good news is it's up to *you* to rewrite that story. So get after it! You can, and you will, if you really want to. But that's your call.

Instead of (insert limiting belief)...
I am choosing (insert new belief—the "reframe").

Repeat this with as many limiting beliefs as you can think of, and see how you feel once you've let it all out and have inserted a new belief in its place.

Pretty straightforward, right? We humans like to overcomplicate plenty of things. This shouldn't be one of them.

It may take time to fully integrate these new beliefs, so be gentle with yourself. I remember hearing someone say, "If you can't believe in yourself right now, that's okay...borrow the beliefs of others until you do," which I love! Another idea is to "act as if." This means, practice stating things as if your belief has already transformed. An example could be, let's say you're applying for a new job and a well-meaning friend says something like, "You don't really have the kind of experience needed to land such a position." Ugh. Your ego is crushed!

But instead of spiraling into your old patterns and thinking, "You're right, I'm definitely under-qualified. I should find something else instead." Try something like, "Thank you for your feedback. I believe in my ability to learn new skills, and I am confident that I would be a great candidate for this job. Having your support would really mean a lot to me."

As I said, this is a practice, which means consciously choosing your thoughts over and over again until they become second nature. And when you mess up, breathe and start again. It's all good!

Understanding Your Triggers

Now that you've begun to get honest about your inner conversations, I want to talk about the infamous topic of *triggers.* We've all got 'em, some more obvious than others.

Emotional triggers are anything that creates an intense emotional reaction, often taking you out of a more positive feeling state. The source of these triggers matters because without knowing that information, it can be hard to heal the root cause, and you'll end up playing an annoyingly frustrating game I call *symptom solution roulette.* It's like putting a bandaid on a broken bone. (Ummm...thank you?) Totally worthless.

Before we dive into triggers, I want to be very clear: triggers can look different for everyone, even if the root appears similar. So when we're looking at our triggers, I want you to look at them through the lens of you and you alone, void of external factors—including people (especially our most loved relationships: partners, children, and caretakers).

Also, how you experience these triggers is deeply personal. So again, don't get caught up in playing the comparison game here either. Honor your own body, emotions, and experiences with grace, love, and compassion.

Some common circumstances that can provoke triggers are:

Feeling abandoned;
Feeling rejected;
Feeling betrayed;
Feeling unlovable;
Feeling unwanted;
Feeling alone/lonely;
Being accused of being "too much" of something (needy, emotional, independent).

You may notice physical symptoms on top of your emotional state as well, such as rapid heartbeat, inability to focus or speak clearly, upset tummy, body temperature changes, acne, digestive distress, headaches, insomnia, even hair loss.

This is where practicing conscious awareness comes in. I like to work backward to better understand how my current state came to be, and how I can solve for any future occurrences. Or at the very least, find a way to diminish the effects they have on me and those around me.

Let's say you planned a special night with your partner. You thought of every last detail, even wearing a scent that you know they love. You set the tone for your date by lighting candles and putting on their favorite music, so when they walk in the door, they'll feel relaxed and loved.

But that's not what happens.

Flustered, they walk in the door a little later than usual, say a quick hello before walking into the bedroom to put on something more comfortable. When they come back out, they notice an open bottle of wine on the counter and pour themselves a glass, asking if you'd like one too. They fail to notice, or at least acknowledge, the music, candles, the fact that the house has obviously been freshly cleaned, or the place settings on the dining room table which you carefully crafted to resemble your first home-cooked meal together.

How does this make you feel? *Defeated? Embarrassed? Unappreciated? Upset? Hurt? Invisible?*

Instead of lashing out, reacting by screaming something you'll likely later regret, *pause.* And follow your feelings backwards.

Think back to a time you felt a similar emotion. Maybe you can trace it all the way back to childhood. Maybe it was something that really bothered you from last week. Whatever the case, it's clear that there is still some unresolved residue surrounding the original event that deserves your love and attention.

This is when you get to take the time to really go there, be present to your inner voice, and *clear the clutter.* In doing so, you avoid reacting from an open wound instead of an open heart.

It's okay to let your partner know that you feel hurt, or whatever your emotions are. What doesn't work is attacking, accusing, or withdrawing, no matter the situation. (I know from personal experience!)

Sure, they may have had a hard day. And no, that's no excuse to be a dick. But also, compassion is a beautiful skill set to harness, and asking questions helps you both to better understand what's really behind their actions (and your triggers). Please note that your feelings are valid because they are true for you, so don't neglect yourself in the process of finding common ground. It's important to not only listen, but to really *hear* what your partner is saying. Which means taking the time to breathe, remove your ego, be present, refrain from interrupting (this is a hard one!) and speak with intention versus reacting. It also means putting aside any distractions, including your racing thoughts that are probably making up some pretty wild stories based on, you guessed it, *your triggers.*

If you want peace, then commit to finding a way to deal with your emotions in a mature and effective manner. This will be a godsend when it comes to enriching any kind of relationship, regardless of the circumstances.

Understanding our triggers is just one piece of the puzzle, but it's an important one. When we understand the origin of these emotions, we can begin using different tools to find what works best for us (I call these "trigger-tamers"). Not only will this allow our nervous system to rest easier, it will provide a more positive experience all around.

Set realistic expectations for yourself, not to be confused with making excuses for unruly behavior! Give yourself grace as you uncover old stories, patterns, and beliefs, and learn coping strategies to show up better for yourself and the world around you.

You've been through some shit. Let compassion be your guide. Like the rest of us circling this big ball of fire, you are constantly evolving. It may feel scary, but I promise you this—it's necessary, if you truly want to experience all that life has to offer.

Let Change Change You

As much as I would love to be able to take the pain, anger, sadness, confusion, and internal struggle away from you, I can't. But just because you're not the same person you were before your trauma occurred, please believe that you are still just as magnificent as you've ever been. Instead of fighting an uphill battle, my encouragement to you is to do whatever you need to do to accept that this is now part of your life and part of your story...and you get to choose how you will use it moving forward.

We tend to hold on so tightly to familiarity; I'm guilty of this at times, too. But the thing about gripping comfort with all our might is that in the process of doing our best to remain the same, we miss the growth that lies within the newness. And with that, we don't allow ourselves to experience the richness beyond our past pain.

Change can be scary. It can also be pretty amazing! I happen to think that a life without change is a big waste of time. There is so much magic available on this human walk, and I don't know about you, but I want to immerse myself in all its senses!

As I stated in Chapter 3, hold onto the gentle reminder that you aren't the same person you were before you were hurt. So yes, needing to find new ways of *being* in the world will be normal—even necessary. Let that be okay. Let this new way of being and seeing and thinking become the drive that moves you forward as you reflect on how far you've come...because you chose not just to survive, but to thrive!

I know you didn't choose this change. Neither did I. But you know what happens when you embrace the unexpected? You open your eyes a little wider until you see the silver lining and with that, you begin to find meaning in the pain. Or possibly, a new meaning for your life altogether.

So lean in, warrior. And let change be the thing that changes you in the best way possible. There's opportunity here, but you've got to be willing to do whatever's necessary to overcome and rise from the ashes. Honestly, I wouldn't take back a single thing about my experience because it led me straight to my purpose, and because of that I am blessed to support courageous and resilient voices in writing their brilliant books, those brave enough to be witnessed as they tell their stories from a place of empowerment versus pain and shame.

These are people just like you.

I do what I do *because* I was raped, and because of my pain. And I am so in-love with my work and my life *because* I chose to keep going.
So don't sell yourself short.
Life is waiting for you to say *yes*, and to show it what you're made of.
So grab hold...
And enjoy the ride!
The only way to find out what's available is to go...all...in!

Is It Possible to Love My Broken Parts?

By now you know my viewpoint on being *broken* (it's not really a thing). Which means, you've probably already guessed that my answer to the question noted above is a resounding *abso-fucking-lutely.*

Instead of running *from* our experiences, I am inviting you to run *toward* them. Because it's in the space between predictability and the unknown that we find our growth point—and we find ourselves.

Perfection is a trap, mainly because it's bullshit. But also because it sets us up for failure, right outta the gate. When we strive for the unattainable jaws of perfection, we end up covering our truth to avoid the sharpness of disappointment in life, and we lose sight of what really matters...our happiness.

We've all experienced a bit of chaos, some of which has proven to be harsh. So find a way to work with the hand you've been dealt—a hand that may have chosen you, *without your permission.*

If you're thinking, "I'm just not there yet," I want you to remember that this is your journey and your process. So if you're still in a place where acceptance seems too far away to wrap your heart around, that's okay, too. Just know that this place of loving yourself, wholly, is available. And when you're ready, it's yours for the taking (refer back to Chapter 2 for a timeline exercise). There's no need to rush your healing. This is to be done on your terms, which means you decide how, when, and where. You choose. And when you do, just know that there are so many people who want to love you through it, if and when you are willing to be held.

If you're somebody who feels alone, and like nobody gets you or could possibly understand, I am sharing some resources in the back of this book for you to check out that have supported me and so many others on our journey home to ourselves. I have no doubt that at least one of them can support you, too. You do not have to do this alone unless you want to. Just remember...

"If you want to go fast, go alone. If you want to go far, go together." – African Proverb

5

Can I Be Courageous Enough to Be Seen?

"We don't heal in isolation, but in community."
– S. Kelley Harrell, Gift of the Dreamtime

I'll never forget the first time I shared my deep, dark secret. I was 23 and had been holding it in for three-and-a-half years when, all of a sudden, sitting next to a man I barely knew, I just couldn't keep it in any longer. Sitting in my living room, I felt the blood rush to my face as my body vibrated and the words tumbled out of my mouth and onto his ears.

With a trembling voice, I let my words breathe out loud for the first time, *"I was raped."*

We'd only met a few weeks prior and this was our second date.

Him: Silence.
Me: Shock.

It was in that moment that I knew what freedom felt like. And I wanted more of it.

He looked at me, clueless what to say next. I could feel his mental wheels turning, searching for the right words, wondering if any were actually needed or was it best to just be still with this information. I felt him read my softening heart as my insides exhaled for the first time in years. Instead of speaking, he wrapped his arms around me, kissed me gently on the forehead and, in that moment, I knew I was safe.

Safe to feel.
Safe to emote.
Safe to share.
Safe to love.
Safe to be witnessed.
Safe to be messy.
Safe to embody my entirety, unapologetically.

Safe. Something I hadn't felt fully since that fateful night—before my body was used and dismissed.

We often keep our secrets to ourselves out of fear whether from...

Judgment.
Shame.
Blame.
Misunderstanding.
Perception.

But what if our secrets are the answer to the healing we desire...the freedom we desire...the life and relationships we desire?

In my experience, secrets keep us sick, sad, and small. I know because I chose to keep my secret hidden for years—and it nearly killed me. I suffered silently, too afraid of being labeled: damaged, broken, weak. I didn't want to be different...but I was. We all are.

Our stories contain pieces that offer hope and healing. And while I feel it's important that we only share what we feel comfortable to share, with people who feel safe, I also believe there's power (and healing) in courage.

The thing about courage, though, is that it's born from confidence, and we obtain confidence through action. Speaking up and allowing ourselves to be seen, raw in our vulnerability while risking the loss of the box we've created around our "everything's fine" exterior, is scary. And it's definitely not the only way to be courageous, although it's a powerful one. But you know what's worse? Silencing our truth and leaving pieces of ourselves to die without a voice. Not to mention the impact we leave on the table by holding our secrets too close, never allowing them to breathe and live outside of us.

It's Not Their Story

Sharing my pain was my first real moment of courageous action, and the very moment that my path became undeniably clear. It was as if the flood gates had opened, my insides came pouring out, and I was left with an empty shell, unsure what was needed to fill myself back up again.

I was lost, absolutely terrified of what breaking my silence would mean during the moment I allowed my truth to pour out of me. My secret was no longer a secret, and there was no turning back now. I was completely exposed. Naked in my humanness, I had shared my big, scary secret with a man I barely knew and yet, I felt lighter than I had in years.

He didn't understand the enormity of what I'd just shared as it pertained to my own healing, nor how his response would affect my ability to be brave moving forward. But that wasn't the point. I didn't need him to get it, I just needed to remove the weight of my truth from my back so I could move on with my life and begin living again, as the new me—the survivor version of me.

From that day forward, my voice became a vessel for hope, driven by the possibility of inspiring healing in others. Nothing could stop me from speaking, not even the nauseous feeling that came every time I opened my mouth to share. And it liberated me in ways I didn't know were possible. Every time I opened my mouth, dry from fear, my voice shook, and I could feel the weight of my story welling up in my throat as if to stop me from being seen and heard all over again. It was like my body wanted me to feel ashamed, while my soul knew there was absolutely nothing to be ashamed about. No matter the terror I felt each and every time the words came pouring out, I continued speaking…and healing…and repeating the process. And I haven't stopped since.

Over the years I have had plenty of people confused by my openness. In fact, in the beginning, my mom (forever my biggest cheerleader) didn't understand why I would share something so deeply personal with the world. But I didn't falter, because deep in my bones I knew that it wasn't about me. Sharing my story was about relating to others and showing them what was possible on the other side of the pain and silence…where healing lived and my new life was waiting. What I learned was that the negative comments, judgment, confusion, and criticism spewed in my direction from others came from their own inner turmoil, possibly fear, and oftentimes, their very own well kept secrets having dealt with something similar.

We don't see things as they are, we see things as *we are*. Which means that every time we feel triggered by another person's words or actions, it's an invitation to go within and ask ourselves, *Why?* More than likely, it has nothing to do with them (or very little, anyway) and everything to do with the unhealed parts of ourselves begging for our attention and care.

Not everyone will understand you. Maybe your truth isn't for them, at least not right now. Regardless, their response is not your responsibility. It's not your job to make others comfortable. It's not your job to make others happy. And it's certainly not your job to make others like you by hiding your true self in the process of seeking validation and approval from trivial external influences.

If you're committed to finding meaning in your pain, and possibly even using your story to create a positive impact, trust that there's a reason you feel called to share such a deeply personal and vulnerable piece of yourself, however you choose to share it with whomever you deem worthy of hearing it. Lean in, shaky lips and all, and don't look back.

While there were (and will continue to be) people turned off by my story, I've had far more people praising my courage than shaming my decision to use my voice. Strangers have come up to me after my talks to share their own secrets for the first time, feeling empowered with a sense of relief to know that they're not alone. This is why I do this work. It's the reason I refuse to allow the opinions of others to halt my inner knowing that I am here with a divine purpose. And I will no longer play small…no matter the discomfort others may feel because of my bigness and my desire to take up space. My voice is here to be heard, just as yours is should you choose to use it.

As humans we want to connect. And it's through our stories that we're able to do so, which requires us to be seen *as we are.*

London, You Stole My Heart

In November of 2018, I was invited to London, England, to be the headline speaker at a two-day women's event. While the focus of the event was female entrepreneurship, they asked if I'd speak specifically about courage and resilience. They wanted me to share my story.

After nearly 13 hours of travel, I landed in what would quickly become one of my favorite cities. The air was crisp, the leaves were changing color, the people were charismatic and friendly. And there happened to be crepes at every café I entered, which I happily indulged in (almost) daily.

As I walked the streets of Chelsea, London, where I was staying, I felt an overwhelming sense of gratitude. I had just *celebrated* the 18th anniversary of my assault that October, and here I was, about to speak to a group of 150+ highly successful women about my experience of being raped and, more importantly, how it had impacted my life in the best way possible. As I strolled through a very old, incredibly beautiful cemetery, tears welled in my eyes, and the familiar lump in my throat before doing something scary made itself known. And just as I encourage my clients to do, I allowed myself to feel it all.

He'd tried to break me, my rapist. And the motherfucker failed! Here I stood, literally halfway around the world, about to spill my heart out in hopes of providing even an inkling of support and encouragement to these women, reveling in the fact that I had been through so much to get to this point.

Trauma can be a tricky little bastard, somehow finding a way to sneak up and bite you in the ass when you least expect it. But I like to think of the scars of trauma as beautiful reminders of how far we've come, and who we've *be*-come in the process of overcoming something that is often incredibly debilitating and confusing to hold.

Unlike rape, where consent is not given, as survivors our perpetrators cannot break our healing spirit without our permission. If you're feeling stuck in muddy waters, waiting to be saved, let me remind you that ***you are the one you've been waiting for.*** Save yourself, for yourself, and for those lucky enough to love you...each and every version of you that has been and will be.

All it took was that one important moment in my living room on that second date with a kind, compassionate man to show me that I was braver than I'd given myself credit for. And that if I let myself continue to be brave, I could use my experience for something meaningful, like helping others on their journey home to themselves through courageous storytelling. I was still walking my own path of healing, and by now I was fully aware that the journey may very well be a lifelong exploration.

The Aftermath of Abandonment

I had begun to tackle my abandonment wounds long before my trip to London. However, the whispers of fear still found their way into my mind from time to time, usually during a moment of insane courage. By now, I was used to this inner chatter but I was sick of it replaying like a broken record, especially because I'd done so much work to get here and I didn't want to hold this unsupportive belief any longer.

People take what they want and they leave me. This was the bullshit babble that filled my brain, giving way to a cesspool of confusion, frustration and resentment. I just wanted to be free. Given the severity of my imprinted memories, it was no wonder that my story of abandonment ran deep within my bones for decades. This belief, which stemmed from my own real-life experiences, felt like a noose around my neck. From my biological father choosing booze and drugs over parenthood before I was born, to my stepfather leaving after the divorce, to being raped, and then having a man I cared for deeply in my thirties disappear after a year and half together without reason or explanation, I had plenty of proof that this story was not only true, but it was personal.

Somewhere within, I held strong to the fear that I was destined to be abandoned, so I should find a way to live with it and stop taking it so personally. But now that I was *different,* I thought the odds were surely that much higher, and it would require a lot of bending and twisting my true self to ensure people stayed.

I was conflicted. On one hand, I knew what I wanted and what I deserved (mostly, anyway). Yet I continued to accept *less than* in an effort to grasp whatever seemed to stick. I was settling for scraps, specifically when it came to men (the model behind my wound), feeling frustrated by my lack of boundaries and wavering self-worth. And because I didn't want anyone to ever feel the sense of abandonment I had so often felt, I found myself staying in situations that didn't serve me, for far longer than I should have, to accommodate *their* needs and wants first. It became a vicious cycle, one that I couldn't seem to pull myself away from. It felt like an addiction, chasing the high of doing whatever necessary to keep the mediocrity from leaving me. Anything felt better than nothing, a dangerous game to play, no matter the context.

When it came to my story of abandonment, and ultimately wanting to prove I was loveable and worthy of a place at the table (in all types of relationships), the desire for safety became my driver while I willingly gave up the wheel.

How much of myself was safe to share? How much of my past was safe to let go? How much bullshit was too much to handle before I'd lose myself in the conquest to stay versus abandon circumstances that didn't serve my highest and best?

Over and over, these questions played in my mind, begging me to face my deepest wounding. Or at least until I was willing to say, *enough is enough already*, which took time. A long time.

The thing is, people are not objects to keep, so when we talk about *losing* someone—can we *lose* something that was never really ours to begin with? The answer is likely somewhere in the gray. However, it's been my experience that the looser the grip, the tighter the bond. What I mean by this is that when we show up as our true selves, those meant for us—both people and experiences—find their way into our experience and as long as there's alignment, the relationship has the opportunity to flourish. It's the Law of Attraction. No matter how hard we want to, we cannot (and should not) try to *make* people stay. Especially at the expense of our own truth and self-worth.

In the end, the real abandonment is that of Self. The abandonment happens when we choose to betray our own heart in hopes of convincing others that we're enough, worthy, or whatever else we are seeking to validate. This will only take us further from our birthright, which is love in all forms, at the deepest level.

Choosing to let people in opens us up to risk. The risk of being hurt. The risk of being left. But most importantly, the risk of being loved—which, as it turns out, is the most brilliant feeling we can possibly experience, both as the giver and the receiver. You don't have to do anything or be anyone other than you to *earn* love. Love is your birthright, no matter what life throws your way. So instead of backing away from the unknown (which can be positive, by the way), move toward it with courage and the belief that what's meant for you will stay...for as long as it's meant to. Anything or anyone that leaves has simply run its course, so find gratitude in the time you had, and keep your heart open to what's trying to make its way to you now that there's room for something new.

Authentic Identification

Part of accepting who you are now is living authentically in that identity. Those who truly loved you before will still love you, they may just need a little help understanding how to love you in the way you need now. You've changed, this is part of being human. And as such, your loved ones may not necessarily know you in the way they once did. This is not your fault or theirs. So instead of filling your heart with anger or resentment, use that same powerful energy to educate them on the newness that is you, whatever that looks like. Just remember that their acceptance (or lack thereof) has absolutely no impact on your worth. Like anything new, this can take a little getting used to as we navigate this fresh, raw territory. Drop the labels, as your experience is neither good nor bad. It just is.

To embody our truth means accepting the path that got us here. Including horrendous acts, positive experiences, and everything else that has played a role in our very existence. We don't have to like all our experiences, but if we choose to accept them for what they are—part of our journey—we can begin to soften into the life waiting for us.

So often we create an identity based on external validation, whether a job title, the amount of money we have in the bank, the size of our house, the brands we wear, the car we drive. But none of that means shit. Not really. If we don't first learn who we are without any of the fluff fogging up the lens of what matters most (our happiness), it becomes far too easy to forget what we're living for in the first place.

It's not the things that bring joy, it's the people. And it starts with us and the relationship we have with our Self.

Getting to know ourselves is a vulnerable endeavor, often uncomfortable if we've never really taken the time to do so. And the only way to know who we are, deep in our bones, is to grant ourselves permission to be honest about our needs, wants, fears, secrets, desires, and everything in between. When we grant ourselves this kind of compassionate permission, we often uncover things we'd hidden away long ago, hoping that by ignoring them, they'd go away. But that's not how memories work. Somewhere, we keep all our moments stored within, and unless we deal with them properly, they're bound to come back up—often at the most inconvenient times.

The more we *stuff* our feelings and experiences, the more crap builds up (I call this mental and spiritual constipation). The key to happiness and inner fulfillment rests within our willingness to go inward and face the demons that have made a home in our darkest parts.

To love ourselves means to honor and accept all of ourselves, no questions asked. We may not like some of the things we've done, words we've spoken, or experiences we've had, but all have formed the person we are now, as well as the person we will ultimately become. Without a doubt, I can tell you this: you are spectacular and deserving of having the most divine human experience available.

But nothing I say can change your inner world—that's completely up to you.

Choose Yourself

In the end, we're all we've got. And I don't mean that in some victim-y, self-loathing sense. Above all else, we know the intricacies of our *being* better than anyone, and it's up to us to be assertive in our quest for our most authentically aligned life. When things get tough—because at some point, they will (it's called living)—always remember to choose *you* first and foremost. This is not selfish, it's necessary if you are to remain in integrity with the truth of your soul.

Pain changes people, and that includes those around us. You cannot take away the experience, and that includes trying to forget that it happened in the first place. So you might as well do what you can to feel it, heal it, and transmute it so that you can move onward and upward.

When we choose ourselves, we create space to let love in. We open ourselves (our heart and our soul), granting ourselves permission to feel safe enough to be *chosen by* as well as to *choose* others. Loving ourselves deeply allows us the capacity to love and be loved just the same.

Can I Be Courageous Enough to Be Seen?

This is a scary one for many, many people, survivors in particular. And it makes sense. Courage, however, is not something we find, it's a practice; one that requires our participation at every turn. So to be courageous we must be willing to say yes to the discomfort. We must be willing to fail and fall. We must be willing to be seen before we are ready to be seen, so long as we feel safe to do so.

Safety is an inside job and requires us to get honest about where we're hiding. Don't let fear be the reason you limit your evolution. There's healing in the unknown. And there are hearts waiting for your courage, the very hearts you're here to inspire.

You have a story...we all do. But pity is a poor man's party. And you are rich beyond measure. So let me ask you this…

What is hiding costing you? Is it worth it?

6

Will I Ever Feel Like I'm Enough?

"We can't hate ourselves into a version of ourselves we can love."
– Lori Deschene

For years after my traumatic experience, I told myself that I was okay. I continued to dive in, do the work, and *follow my bliss* the best I could, something my Nana always encouraged me to do. While I did a great job of appearing like everything was okay, deep inside I felt a lingering sense of disconnection that scared me. An observer in my own experience, I began noticing the ways in which I was compensating for the work yet to be done—the work I was unconsciously avoiding, filling the space instead with busy-ness, shaky boundaries, and subsequent burnout.

As hard as I tried, I couldn't quite muster the energy to come face to face with the unresolved emotional turmoil swirling around in my soul. I was so sick of *feeling* all the time. Yet it's who I was (and still am), and on some level that frustrated me. A feeler at my core, I thrive in the unknown caverns of existence, often diving into the depths of discomfort as a way to better understand and connect with others as well as myself. I long to understand *why*, a question that drove my mom crazy when I was a kid, but one that has since served me well. Maybe it's my Scorpio side, or maybe it's a byproduct of being raised in an environment where my curiosity was encouraged. Whatever the case, I was tired of it all, and I just wanted things to be easy...even if only temporarily.

Comparison Kills More Dreams Than Failure Ever Will

On some level, I felt like I had been struggling to stay afloat my entire life. As a kid, I struggled with confusing emotionally charged outbursts, which I now know is due to the deep-seated (unconscious) anger I felt from the absence of my father and desiring more quality time and attention from my hard-working single mom. I struggled to feel safe in my own body, which I believe stemmed first from early parental abandonment that continued to show up repeatedly in my relationships with male authority figures and "role models." I struggled to say what I really wanted to say in its entirety due to my fear of being abandoned (again) for saying the "wrong" thing. I struggled with my health after being raped, which really pissed me off because I took pride in how well I took care of myself, yet my body didn't want to cooperate. I struggled financially, the result of giving away my gifts for peanuts, seeking validation and acceptance in place of resentment. I struggled to receive love...because somewhere inside, I questioned my enoughness.

As I watched others seemingly skate through life, I couldn't help but wonder, *Why was I always struggling and they weren't?* Looking back, I played the victim—although silently, which is hard for me to admit. What did I know, anyway? Maybe they *were* struggling, but like me, they were also doing so under the radar. I made assumptions about others' paths based on the version of themselves they were allowing the world to see. Was it a mask? Maybe. But it didn't matter because none of it was my business and shouldn't have affected me. But it did. Because I let it.

The challenge for me was confronting my conditioning and realizing that it was okay to admit I was struggling. Even that felt hard. Likely because I was raised to look on the bright side, and find the silver lining in everything, something I am so grateful for. But, the truth was that deep down, I was frustrated and, quite frankly, annoyed that nothing seemed to go my way no matter how hard I tried—a reality that felt lonely and unfair. I harbored resentment toward the people who took advantage of me, neglecting my own responsibility in the role I played in the outcome, the repercussions of which resulted in stress, chronic inflammation, and eventually serious and debilitating illness.

No matter how hard I pushed (or, forced—masculine energy), it felt like my efforts somehow found a way to come crashing down around me, suffocating me in the process of searching for simplicity (or, flow—feminine energy). Maybe I was just meant to live a challenging life, by first-world standards. Maybe it was my destiny to struggle. Maybe the lessons I was here to learn in this lifetime were exactly that, and I was actually on the right track. And I resented the fuck out of that possibility, too.

I didn't see it at the time, but I was in a perpetual state of comparison, thinking that if I did what he/she did, I would inevitably get the same (positive) results. But that's not what happened. Ever. (If you're familiar with human design, I'm a projector so in retrospect, the "struggling" I was constantly facing makes total sense! People like us are meant to pave a new way for others to follow. We are the "seers," the wayshowers here to guide and direct energy and sometimes, it's a tiresome responsibility to accept and uphold.)

Instead, I was focusing on my external environment to get the internal results I craved, and it was not working. I was *forcing* outcomes instead of allowing *flow* to unfold, an exhausting and toxic pattern that I was eventually able to release...years later, after hitting my very own rock bottom.

Your Brain on Trauma

Aside from being holed up in a hospital bed over the span of nine years in my twenties, and spending a good portion of the remaining time I had with my head in medical books trying to heal myself, I now had a term for my memory loss surrounding my assault: *dissociative amnesia,* a common and curious side effect of trauma.

Dissociative amnesia is when a person loses memory as a way to cope with the event(s). It's the body's brilliant way of self-preservation and self-protection. The strange part for me was that it wasn't the event itself that I had forgotten—I can still recall those details clearly. It was a chunk of years prior to, and post-rape, that escaped me.

For so long, I didn't have a name for those missing memories or understand what was happening. All I knew was that I was different, and I had to come to terms with the reality that I may never get my memories back. I needed to find a way to be okay with these "missing pieces" if I wanted to move forward, which I have since been able to manage with compassion and care.

So let's talk about post traumatic stress disorder (PTSD) for a hot minute. PTSD comes from a lack of *resourcing* available by the individual, which leads to overwhelm and the shutting down or inability to process the traumatic event(s). Resourcing, or *the awareness of and ability to utilize accessible tools*, is key to regulating our nervous system and its response or reaction to circumstances. Somatic experiencing (SE) was something that kept coming up as I was looking for support. I'd tried so many different modalities, but nothing quite tackled the root of the problem the way I'd hoped. Eventually, I began toying with the fundamentals of SE, diving into my body (soma) as a way to better understand its role in "whole-self" healing. Talk about profound realizations! We truly can be our own healers when armed with the right tools.

Our body wants to keep us safe. How the body attempts this involves multiple factors including past programming, as well as our ability to access (and willingness to visit) our truth and take a look at our present-day beliefs and habits. Of course, it's more complex than that. But for the sake of this book, and the fact that I am not a trained therapist or psychologist, I'm speaking in basic terms to get the point across. Our bodies are highly intelligent and operate through the lens of safety, which means they will do whatever is necessary to create equanimity…whether we're consciously participating or not.

In 2015, I completed my 200-hour yoga teacher training, in search of a deeper way to connect inward and discover any unhinged pieces still floating around. I had just left an 11 year relationship (with the man I mentioned earlier, the first person I'd shared my secret with) so my heart was tender. I was in *aaaaallllllll* the feels when I decided to embark on this journey back to myself—and then it hit me.

I am choosing this stuck-ness. I am choosing this disconnection. I am choosing this pain. But why?

As I sat with these questions, I allowed the deep inner whispers to come forth. As much as I wanted to swat the answers away, I knew it was time to stand up to my ego and get honest with myself. I had spent so many years struggling. And on some level, the struggle, while uncomfortable, made me feel safe. It was familiar. I understood it. Yet it frustrated me beyond belief.

As it turns out, I had become addicted to the struggle. Even now, I'm still learning to release lingering remnants of this story steeped in struggle while simultaneously choosing to create a new reality for myself. It's conscious work. It's moment-by-moment work. And when I'm not paying attention, it can still creep up, often disguising itself as a warm fuzzy blanket inviting me to curl up and get comfortable… right before it attacks!

Studies show that for many of us self-proclaimed "struggle addicts," when things are going well, we find ways to sabotage. Complaining. Overthinking. Overanalyzing. Making excuses. Procrastinating. Blaming. Ignoring the flashing red lights in our face screaming, *Warning! Warning!* For me, it's typically a racing mind in the middle of the night, leading to insomnia, which lends itself to low energy and an inability to function at my highest potential.

I tell you this because I know there are plenty of others out there who are caught up in a similar trap. Yet, we don't have to stay here, and this certainly doesn't have to be our "normal" way of operating in the world. We deserve better. To align with our deepest desires, we must show up better and learn how to let go of anything weighing us down. Speaking from experience, it can feel really frustrating to desire one thing and get another, especially when you feel like you're *doing all the things* you know to do. But at the end of the day, *the feedback is the feedback.* We get what we put out. Do not confuse this with blaming others for our shitty outcomes! *We* are responsible for our lives.

All I'm saying is that when things aren't working out in ways that feel good for us, it's time to look in the mirror and have a come-to-Jesus moment, our own little awakening. It's time to get honest and do what needs to be done to pivot and recalibrate. We may not be able to control everything that happens, but we can absolutely control how we respond and react in any given situation. This is the power of the mind.

After completing a 60-hour training course with The Embody Lab in 2021, I received my certification in Integrative Somatic Trauma Therapy. All these years later, I am still learning to trust myself, and my body. But it's been through cultivating a conscious practice *with* my body, *for* my body, that I am now able to bounce back quicker, with more compassion. If you're not there yet, that's okay! Remember, this is your process, nobody else's. One moment at a time. One day at a time. One breath at a time. Eventually, you will overcome. And when that happens, promise me you'll celebrate.

The Mindful Garden

"With our minds we create the world." – Buddha

When I was a kid, I used to spend a lot of time at my grandma's house during the weekdays each summer while my mom was working. Most mornings, I'd wrinkle my nose in confusion as I looked out the window to see my Nana contorted in weird positions, mouthing gibberish to herself on a freshly cut patch of green grass, surrounded by her beloved garden. I now know this as yoga and meditation, something that seemed like a solid waste of time as a kid. My Nana was always ahead of her time though, and this was clearly no exception.

I'd questioned her many times, wondering why on earth she would spend so much time in silence, chanting, or talking to the trees. "Sheree, yoga and meditation allow us to come home to ourselves, and reconnect to our mind and body. The real waste of time is the junk between our ears!" With my Nana, everything came back to mindset, as well as the power we all possess to create our reality based on our thoughts and, subsequently, our actions. She believed forming a healthy, positive mindset was made easier by taking the time to pause, silence our inner chatter, and be with the truth of our soul. It took me a while to fully comprehend what she meant. But as time went on, I began to understand the depth of her words. She was right (of course she was). And never would her wisdom be so profoundly impactful than after the rape and all the years that followed.

Bali, Baby!

During yoga teacher training, I made a decision that would impact my life forever. Not only was I tending to a broken heart at the time, but I had just stepped into a brand new life as a single woman on my own, and I felt as if my eyes were opening for the first time. Training was set to wrap up in November, which happens to be my birth month, so I thought, *Why not do something big to celebrate all the newness of this past year?!*

I'd heard so many people talk about Bali, especially in the yoga community. So I Googled it, and like so many others who've done the same thing, I was sold! I booked my ticket to leave a couple weeks after training was over, and I decided to travel around Indonesia *by myself* for nearly a month. Part of me thought I'd gone a little bananas, but the other part of me, the *truth* of me, knew this was exactly what I needed.

I'd never traveled alone internationally before, but the thought of exploring a new place, without an agenda and *on my terms*, felt exhilarating. I hopped on the train, which took me from San Diego to Los Angeles, where I'd booked a flight to Denpasar, Indonesia, with a four hour layover in Taipei, Taiwan. I brought my laptop so I could still do some work while I was away, successfully (and illegally) sublet my adorable studio in the heart of Hillcrest (San Diego), and packed one large travel backpack before heading out on my first solo adventure. This would also be the first time I would spend Christmas alone away from my family, which felt a little strange. However, I knew this was the right decision for me, and it was clear that my soul needed space to do some serious searching.

Sitting in the Taipei airport, I noticed a woman who looked to be about my age typing away on her laptop. She appeared to be alone as well, which made me feel a little more settled about my decision to fly across the world with just a backpack and my healing heart. She later approached me and asked if I would watch her stuff while she ran to the bathroom, which I was happy to do (also a big TSA no-no but such is the life of a couple of rebels). When she returned, we got to chatting and formed an instant friendship.

Her name was Louise, and she was traveling solo from San Francisco to Bali for a month. What a coincidence! We seemed to have a lot in common, and the conversation felt easy. I was drawn to her calming, open energy, and her similar sense of humor. We exchanged numbers on WhatsApp and decided we'd try to meet up once we got settled into our respective accommodations. Already, the alignment of saying *yes* to my soul was paying off.

I'll never forget stepping off the plane and walking into the humidity, with my backpack in tow, to find an adorable Indonesian man holding a sign with my name on it. I'd hired a driver for my trip, as I'd heard horror (and hilarious) stories about getting around in Bali, and I was definitely not interested in learning how to drive a scooter through their very busy streets. I was not, however, prepared for the wild ride that was to come. I mean, how there aren't more accidents in Indonesia is astonishing to me. Let's just say I felt like I was on the most intense roller coaster ride of my life, without a safety belt, having every sensory experience possible thrown at me, namely shrieking car horns and erratic brake lights! I'm pretty sure I got whiplash on the ride from the airport to Ubud, where I was beginning my trip. But I giggled with joy and fascination the whole way.

Stranded

I spent the first couple of days getting my bearings. I'd originally booked the same villa for my entire trip thinking I could cancel at any point if I wanted a change of scenery; at least this would give me a home-base. My intention for the trip was relaxation, exploration, and healing, so the listing for Villa Mantra Bali, aside from me not being a vegan, sounded like utter perfection!

"Welcome spiritual warriors…6 private bedrooms and a 4 capsule shared women's dorm room, pool & yoga studio. We're located a 5 min via scooter from central Ubud. Join us for cacao ceremonies around the fire, kirtans, meditations & dinners out with the tribe. Know where to go & what's happening from a yogi insider/vegan foodie.

The villa is a touch of rustic modern, Japanese tatami living, open air and spacious. There is plenty of room to practice yoga, meditate, work online or lounge around. We have a new fire pit in the garden and film projector for movie nights. Referrals and repeat guests are our foundation. Many of my closest friends were first met here as guests. It's a great place to meet and learn the in's and out's of Ubud from someone who is part of that scene. We have staff that sweep rooms, common space, garden and the pool 4-5 days a week."

I arrived in the dark and found a note with my name on it along with instructions to enter my private villa, which faced the outdoor open kitchen and courtyard/pool area. While my room was adorable and the quaint grounds were beautiful and lush, I quickly learned that it was much further from town than I'd anticipated, despite the description. I'd booked it with the impression that I could easily walk everywhere based on my conversations with the community liaison, because as I said, there was no way I was going to jump on a scooter on my own. And I suppose that was technically true, I could have walked (and I did...*once)*, but it was not exactly a walkable area given the literal holes in the sidewalks (like, fall into the abyss kind of holes, with no way out). Add in the humidity and lack of respectful street etiquette (in the form of obnoxious cat calls), and walking to and from town was quite an alarming experience for a tourist traveling alone in a foreign country.

I ended up flagging down a driver on my walk back to my villa the *one day* I attempted the trek. He did not speak the slightest bit of English but seemed to understand when I showed him the address where I was going, so I hopped on the back of his scooter and held on for dear life. As we zig-zagged up the chaotic, pot-hole-ridden roads, it was clear to me he was a little confused as to where we were headed, and I could feel the panic rising in my throat.

"Sir, are you sure this is the right way?" He mumbled something under his breath, seemingly frustrated by my question. By now I was certain we'd passed my villa. As I looked around the vast landscape whipping by me, I realized we were in the middle of nowhere...without another living being in sight.

Surrounding us were lush rice paddy fields with a few modest homes spread about, but for the most part, we seemed to be completely alone. As we approached what appeared to be a small market of sorts, I asked him to pull over so I could get directions. He seemed annoyed by my request and huffed while mumbling something under his breath yet again, as he veered his scooter to the side of the road before coming to an abrupt stop.

"I'll just be a minute. I want to run inside and make sure we're going the right way. Thank you so much for stopping...I'll be right back."

As I walked up the short drive, I heard the sound of wheels screeching just as I turned around to see my driver peeling out, leaving me deserted. Shocked, I scurried up to the front door only to realize that this "market" was nothing but a vacant property, with nothing around for miles. I may have peed my pants a little before frantically grabbing my phone.

No service. Zero. *What the actual fuck?* I was totally stranded...and I began to cry.

Now let me preface this by saying, I am horrible with directions. Like, the worst. And given that I had never been to this place before, I certainly had no idea where I was or how to get home, directionally challenged or not. Everything around me looked exactly the same!

I took a moment, closed my eyes, exhaled a few deep breaths, prayed to the heavens and asked for guidance. Then I waited. No scooters passed, no people either. While I felt helpless and terrified, I didn't have much of a choice. I needed to figure this out quickly, or I was sure I would die from heatstroke, or some sort of wildlife attack/insect bite. (Of course, this was just anxiety speaking...I was totally fine, although sweating profusely and really freaking thirsty!)

I retraced our drive from town to where I'd been dropped off and left to die. Okay, that's a bit dramatic. But I was nearly pissing myself with fear! I knew that we'd started our drive heading the right way, which was behind me, so I turned around and began walking in the direction I believed we'd come from, hoping I was right.

All in all, I walked a good two to three miles before things started to look familiar, and I felt an inkling of hope and relief wash over me. I spent the next hour in silence, repeating *I am safe* in my head as I followed my intuition, trusting it would lead me back to my villa in one piece. Which, thankfully, it did. Then I cried again, although this time in relief, before collapsing on my bed and thanking the Universe for its help, vowing to move locations as soon as possible, somewhere closer to town where I could easily walk to and from wherever I wanted to go. But first, I needed to calm down and reset my nervous system. As you can probably imagine, I was a bit of a mess.

My villa happened to be next door to a spa, which was very modest and unlike anything I'd seen in the states. After indulging in one of the most incredible massages of my life in hopes of combating the jetlag still clinging to me, I recommitted to having an amazing adventure moving forward, regardless of what had just happened. I said I wanted memorable so...thank you? (I can laugh about it now, but it was incredibly scary at the time!)

Now get this. These massages, which I am pretty sure were made from baby tears and unicorn manes, cost me a whopping $11 USD for 90-minutes of absolute bliss including tip, which is not expected due to the 21% tax added to most goods/services. They were pure magic and dirt cheap and as such, I spent the next month getting daily rub-downs from the small albeit mighty hands of the Balinese women as I bounced around Indonesia. This gem of a find was definitely a highlight on my trip. The manicures and pedicures, however, were another story! I'll save you from all the details but to paint a picture (no pun intended), think 100% humidity, while having your nails painted outside where it was very windy with debris flying everywhere, only to have them finish the job with a hot Conair blow dryer, which never actually dried the polish at all. Needless to say, I left with dirt and leaves stuck to my toes. Welcome to Bali, baby!

That was only the beginning of the many stories accumulated throughout that trip, some more uplifting than others. I had not quite anticipated the challenges I'd face when it came to the really important work of learning to quiet my mind long enough to allow stillness to consume me. Turns out I had quite an aversion to the void, which I'd never realized previously. This meant I still had a lot of work to do to find the healing I sought.

The Pain of Stillness

We often think that stillness means reading a book or watching a show or relaxing with friends by the pool. But stillness in the way that I'm sharing here has nothing to do with *doing* anything, but rather, doing *nothing* as a way to gain a deeper understanding of ourselves.

And herein lies the discomfort.

It's been my experience, likely due to the world we live in, that true stillness is often mislabeled as laziness. We've grown accustomed to *going* and *doing* constantly, instead of stopping to be present with ourselves, without all the distractions and expectations that we, often unknowingly, make a priority over our own self-care and sanity.

Social media, email, text messages, WhatsApp, Voxer, TikTok...the list is endless! I know that when I really allow myself to disconnect to reconnect, I always feel lighter, happier, more in tune with myself and those around me. But how often do we really give ourselves permission to pause, and say *no* to obligations or expectations that don't actually feel aligned with what we know we need? For many of us the answer is a solid: hardly ever (or never).

Since taking that first of (now) many solo trips abroad, I've gotten much better at shutting out the noise of the world in order to go within. In the beginning, that shit was hard, and I avoided it at all costs. I truly believed that to succeed in life and business, I needed to run myself into the ground to prove my worth and earn my keep. It was horribly unhealthy and, in many ways, ineffective. Sure, I was opening doors to some incredible opportunities to be part of some really impactful work. But much of it was at the expense of my health and happiness. I felt fulfilled in many ways, but deep down I knew this lifestyle was unsustainable, which terrified me.

I mistook stillness for slowing down, although still *doing* in the process. For a while, I was really proud of myself when I took a day off, including my weekends, which I typically spent with my nose in my computer writing! For years, I worked myself to the bone, never asking for more money to compensate for my time and effort, not to mention the finished product I provided my clients, which was exceptional. I felt underappreciated, taken advantage of—and, in turn, I became resentful. Yet I was to blame, not them. I had taught people how to treat me, and I'd accepted *less than* out of fear of being cut off and abandoned...my greatest fear of all. So of course this was the outcome, but it didn't make me feel any better.

So uncomfortable in my own stillness, I ignored any signs begging me to take a break and rest. I mean, *really rest.* Embracing stillness was such a foreign concept that it went against everything I'd been raised to believe. Things like...

You have to work really hard to make good money.
Money is hard to make, and harder to keep.
Only people who work 24/7 become financially successful.
Success and wealth are for lucky people.
You've gotta take whatever job pays the bills; it's nearly impossible to make money doing what you love.
Rich people are assholes.
More money, more problems.

I've since learned via the proof of many successful friends, clients and colleagues, that these beliefs are not only wrong, but they are outdated ways of thinking. In truth, abundance manifests through alignment (including working smarter, not harder).

Yes, having a strong work ethic is imperative. And yes, spending time mastering your craft so you can provide an amazing product and/or service to the world is required.

But it's *false* that you've gotta kill yourself to simply make ends meet, let alone attract abundance and create a fulfilling career you truly love with money in the bank and an ability to give back and experience life however you choose.

Real wealth begins within, and financial wealth is cultivated through the alignment of skills, purpose, passion, service, and leadership. For so long, I had such a hard time trusting my decisions because of my past (like saying *yes* to a date with the man that would ultimately rape me). So instead of asking for help, delegating tasks to a team, or saying *no* when the project didn't feel right, I said *yes* to nearly every single thing that came my way, leaving no room for stillness, or anything else.

It wasn't until I left my long-term relationship and lived in a home by myself that I grasped what stillness really meant. There was nobody to talk to. There was nobody to cook for and enjoy meals with. Being alone with myself gave "space" a whole new meaning. And although I knew space was exactly what I needed, I couldn't help but feel guilty for indulging.

Bali changed all of that for me. Mama Bali, as she's often referred to, gave me permission to not only slow down, she gave me permission to *stop* and truly be present with myself in a way I hadn't ever recalled experiencing before.

I wrote in my journal every day. I took long walks through town and drank freshly pressed juice every day. I worked on silencing my mind, using guided meditation as a vehicle for stillness, every day. And I practiced yoga every day. This new daily practice became about *progress*, and instead of beating myself up for not doing it perfectly, I reframed my automatic judgment. Instead of criticizing myself, I focused on gratitude, because I was finally allowing myself to recognize just how much I had to be thankful for.

This was the beginning of a new chapter in my life, starting in Bali. One that involved stepping further into my voice and asserting boundaries without guilt, although there were a lot of ups and downs in the process. Having this sacred time to myself invited me to finally release the pain I'd unknowingly been holding onto, while being intentional in cultivating a life that was all mine.

Resilience and Gratitude

"Service to others is the rent you pay for your room here on earth." – Unknown

After taking a short three-to-four-day trip to Gili Trawangan, which was about a 50-minute car ride from Ubud to Sanur Harbor, Louise, Ashlee and I made our way back to Ubud, where I'd landed in yet another villa within town. A few days later, the three of us decided to meet up for lunch at Art Kafé near Monkey Forest, before getting a ride with our new (and very fun) driver, Agung, to *Yayasan Widya Guna*, a formal non-profit organization just outside of Ubud, to bring rice and balloons to the kiddos.

This was the first time I volunteered on vacation, something I have since implemented on all of my subsequent solo adventures abroad. The entire experience was rewarding and impactful, for all of us. To see the smiles on all of their faces...my heart was forever changed. I think theirs were, too.

Yayasan Widya Guna was founded by Ketut Sadia and Gill Rijnenberg, who opened their doors in 2006. Their mission began in one small room in their home, where they welcomed 12 orphans and a few very poor children from the village of Bedulu. They started by teaching the children English. Word spread quickly, and a few years later, with the help of donations, an entire compound was built out of recycled wood, and they established a real school. Since then, their numbers have increased to 100+ students due to the number of disadvantaged children living locally, as well as the organization's open-armed philosophy. This philosophy says, *There's always room for one more.* Their school is unique in that they accept handicapped students as well as able-bodied children, which other surrounding schools did not (at least not during our time there).

The founder was kind enough to give us a tour of the grounds when we arrived. I was amazed to see that they had an organic garden, where the kids learned to grow and care for their own food—this resonated so deeply with my core beliefs and made my soul sing. Walking around the outdoor campus, we peaked in on a teacher giving a lesson to a small classroom of students on the importance of healthy food. Fitness was also part of their program and when we arrived, kids were playing "futbol" in the front entrance.

As we made our way around the compound, we found a group of about 12 students, ages 5–13, preparing for a Christmas musical. They were to perform for guests and locals on Christmas Eve where they'd be singing 10 songs in English. Learning to speak English was a very important component of their studies, as the school wanted to give the kids the best chance at succeeding once they left.

The teachers were primarily volunteers from all over the world, who typically came for three months at a time. Many of these kind and thoughtful people were regular volunteers, coming yearly to support the foundation and the children by teaching the kids and also paying for their food and lodging as a way to give back and support the school's mission.

The students of *Yayasan Widya Guna* are sponsored by people from all over the world, with 100% of the donations going to the kids. Whatever money they are given by their sponsor is documented, and the students have to keep a record of everything spent—books, supplies, etc.—for school. Each year, they present this to their sponsor so the sponsor knows where their money is going and so the kids learn how to balance money. I wish I learned that in school! The money from the sponsors, as well as the money made from the volunteer teachers, help to keep everything running smoothly and efficiently.

The children were so polite and adorable, coming up to us asking, *"Hello, what is your name?"* Followed by, *"My name is (fill in the blank), where are you from?"* Their English was on point. This was such a humbling and heart-warming experience...one that I feel so blessed to have been a part of.

We learned so much from the Balinese children and their teachers. They were kind, humble, warm, inviting, open, and curious. They didn't have much, yet they were genuinely happy. I could see the impact the school had on their growing confidence and desire to do something important and fulfilling in the world. They shared their dreams for the future with us, which would undoubtedly be bright.

After hearing the stories of where many of them had come from, and then seeing the way they laughed and played and interacted with their peers as well as us—*three foreign strangers*—I couldn't help but smile at their resilience and sheer willpower to rise above all the turmoil and setbacks. Children are magical in this way, and I often wonder at what point do we shift from seeing the world through the lens of love to being hardened by our experiences and fearful of what's outside?

Many of these kids had been severely abused, starved, abandoned, even left for dead. But when given the opportunity to change their circumstances, with the help of some amazing earth angels, they took it with open arms. I have no doubt that for some of them the transition was hard. And based on what the founder shared, not everyone adapted right away. Yet with time, showered with love and consistency by adults that truly cared about their well-being, they flourished. We can do this, too, but we've gotta open our hearts for this to be possible.

These beautiful little ones inspired me in so many ways, reaffirming my belief that healing is possible for us all. We all have the capacity for resilience, even if we haven't fully embodied how to project that resilience outward through our thoughts and actions. We often hold ourselves back from the life waiting for us out of fear or the lack of belief that it's possible for us because (insert your own story)—paired with the unwillingness to take the big, scary action necessary to realize our dreams. But none of that is true.

We are all capable and worthy of achieving wholeness again, no matter what we've been through. We must want the glory more than we want to hold onto the pain, though, for this to be a reality. When we decide we want more, and take the actions necessary to align to that truth, the whole world will conspire in our favor. That's simply how it works.

Will I Ever Feel Like I'm Enough?

Do you ever look around and think, *"Holy shit…I made it!"* If not, I highly suggest you give it a try. Because you're still here, and that tells me you are fierce, determined, and resilient. Through all the craziness and potential traumas you've experienced in your life, something inside you was committed to keep going. Take a minute and give yourself some credit. Life can be hard! But that doesn't mean we quit.

We are all flawed. But just the same, as Brené Brown says, we are all *worthy of love and belonging.* We need to stop hating ourselves into *enoughness*…it doesn't work like that. Love is what will set us free, and it begins with our willingness to first love ourselves.

Here are some questions to ask yourself as you dive into the root of your beliefs and discover what needs to change to further align to the life you're working so hard to create…

What makes you believe you're not enough?
Who told you that you needed to earn your keep (your worth was dependent on it)?
Are you willing to drop any outdated beliefs to make room for better feeling beliefs to take up space?
When you think about the life you want, what does it look, feel, smell, and taste like? (Write these things down and put them somewhere you can see them every day.)

You are enough. You have always been enough. No amount of trauma, pain, mistakes, or anything else can change that. Feeling and truly believing you're enough, on the other hand, is an inside job. And no amount of external validation, approval, accolades, or anything else can change that.

If you want to embody the confidence of enoughness, commit to stillness and coming home to yourself in whatever way you need to shift, transform, and evolve into the version of yourself that wants to come out to play. She is worthy, just as you are now. Love her, and remind her she's not alone.

7

Can I Be Brave Enough to Speak My Truth?

"Anything that's human is mentionable, and anything that is mentionable can be more manageable. When we can talk about our feelings, they become less overwhelming, less upsetting, and less scary. The people we trust with that important talk can help us know that we are not alone." – Fred Rogers

The first time speaking out, as with anything, can be an incredibly scary experience. During that second date I mentioned earlier, I had not intended to tell the guy I had practically just met about my big scary secret. But sometimes, it's in the space of safety that these brave moments find us, allowing us to step further into our desired healing and growth. As the words clumsily tumbled out, I felt my throat fighting to constrict to protect my truth. But I had already leaped, and there was no turning back.

Sharing such a personal piece of information left me trembling, as my eyes fought back tears. Whether those tears were for the girl who had been violated just a few years prior, or the woman standing courageously before this man exposing the depth of her "damage" without any sort of filter, I wasn't sure. Yet it was there that my deepest secret and reality collided, and I was left with my story spilled out on the floor, messy and raw, revealing pieces of myself that had transformed all that I was and would ultimately become.

I was raised to speak up and take up space yet, as I got older, the world showed me differently. There had been so many times where my "bigness" (despite my petite frame) was "too much." At the time, I took that to mean I needed to water down pieces of myself to be accepted. I now know that's total bullshit, and I don't care one bit about being accepted by people who don't care to understand me in the first place. I'm not for those people, just as you will not be for everyone either. So when the truth finds your lips and asks to be heard, open your mouth and let 'er rip!

Take up space, warrior. Nothing (nobody) can silence you any longer. Not without your permission. Just remember, you hold the power to experience the best that life has to offer. And no matter what you've been led to believe, it's possible to get on the other side of the pain in one piece.

Latchkey Kid

Growing up in a single-parent home had its ups and downs, as one might imagine. Of course, as a kid, I didn't understand the sacrifices being made on my behalf and often acted out as a way to get attention from my mom. She worked so hard for us, something I can appreciate deeply now that I'm an adult. But as a child, all I knew was that I wanted more time with my mom, and not having it left me frustrated and confused.

From as far back as I can remember, it was ingrained in me to be independent and rely on nobody but myself. "You don't need anyone, especially a man, Sheree! You can do it all on your own." Words spoken with conviction from my sweet Nana; words that echoed in my head constantly into adulthood. While well-intended, those very sentiments created a series of unfortunate choices as a result of the literal meaning I had adopted. Independence (which in my case showed up as an unhealthy amount of self-reliance), as I understood it, meant success—and I was determined to succeed!

I grew up with a mom who was always very nurturing and supportive, but she was absent a lot, spending countless hours at work to make ends meet and give us (me in particular) the best life possible. She succeeded brilliantly in that realm, as I never felt a sense of lack when it came to new clothes for school or the ability to enroll in whatever sports or extracurricular activities that interested me. What she couldn't provide in the way of quality time she made up for with, what I believe became, overcompensation of *stuff* (not to be confused with getting my way all the time, that certainly wasn't the case). This dynamic puzzled me, and when I moved away for college, it became apparent that I had not been taught the real importance of having a healthy relationship with self-care (especially rest), personal boundaries (saying *no*), or money. Lessons I would later learn the hard way. I don't fault her for any of this, as she did the best she could and remained an incredible mother, mentor and friend.

By the age of 10, I was home alone quite a bit, meaning that along with getting my school work done before bed, food also became something I took charge of for myself. Let's just say all the low-carb-toting health pros out there would be appalled by my meal choices (spaghetti and ramen on repeat...frozen veggies and canned soup...boxed cereal). It all served a purpose. I mean, I was never hungry. But after my assault, my perspective on "food as medicine," a philosophy my grandmother talked about constantly, completely changed. I realized just how important food really was to our overall health, as well as our healing.

As a kid, I kept busy with soccer and dance. As I grew into my teens, I gave both of those things up and swapped them for running track through junior high, moving onto becoming a varsity cheerleader in high school, fully engaged in everything possible when it came to school spirit with a jam-packed social calendar. I was surrounded by love, yet I craved something more. I was always the person who friends came to for advice, especially when it came to boys! I had a pretty steady boyfriend from 7th grade until my senior year of high school, when we finally broke up for good and I experienced my very first heartbreak.

I was always someone who spoke up and I encouraged others to do the same. I was far from shy, yet I had a real sense of needing alone time in order to come back to myself and recharge. Even as a kid, I felt others' pain deeply. It was challenging to understand, and I didn't know how to articulate it, let alone manage it. I remember coming home from large gatherings feeling so exhausted for what seemed like no reason at all. Looking back, my teens were really the point where my empath nature made itself known. But it wasn't until my thirties that I really understood what that meant, and I began to honor my energetic boundaries as a means for not only survival but expanding my ability to thrive and serve.

Pack Mule Manifested

Growing up is fucking weird. Adulthood included! I remember thinking that my mom had it all figured out while she was raising me—which, now that I've done the whole "adulting" thing, is pretty laughable. I've come to the conclusion that nobody really knows what they're doing, and we're all just figuring it out as we go. But it took me making my own mistakes to realize that we're all a bit wobbly at best on our paths toward whatever it is we desire. And it's in the uncertainty of our journeys that makes for the most beautiful of destinations.

It wasn't until I hired a trauma coach in the Fall of 2021 that I saw how intertwined my past "roles" had become in how I was experiencing my current reality. As we dug into inner child work, and the pain I had not acknowledged was still present, I began to see the unconscious patterns I'd covered up as a way to shield and protect myself. And, in a way, to protect my mom, too.

I believe the responsibilities I was given early on helped me become the driven woman I am today. But there's something to be said for allowing a kid to be a kid. For some households, such as mine, that's simply not an option. And I recognize that there's no shame in that at all—it can be quite liberating, actually. Yet because I was asked to grow up a bit quicker than many of those around me, I developed a sense of over-responsibility and thus over-protection for those I loved. After the rape, I felt this grasp tighten, holding onto things and people I should've let go of, even when it hurt.

For so long I had carried the weight of others' pain and sorrow, unaware of how to release it from my body and free myself from the shackles I'd become so used to wearing. I was a pack mule of secrets and stories. And to some degree, I took pride in this role.

But through the work with my coach, I was able to see the detriment I was causing to my own expansion and, as such, the disservice I was doing to the very world I was committed to elevating. I was part of the problem, which meant I could also be part of the solution.

By recognizing my actions that had become second-nature, it became so clear why I struggled to remain energized after interacting with certain people. My unconscious desire to care for the well-being of others, seeing this as my responsibility *so they wouldn't leave me* (unconscious belief), was staring me straight in the eyeballs, and I had nowhere to hide any longer. So I faced it. I restructured my boundaries, had some hard conversations, and asked loved ones for what I needed to feel supported and cared for. I allowed myself to once again be in the practice of receiving.

The pieces of my soul that had been watered down (with my unconscious permission through my actions) began to bloom anew. I found myself coming home to the woman within, who was also the lost little girl who had been craving love while seeking it outside herself for so long.

Here I am, sweet girl. Remember me? Please forgive me for abandoning you. Thank you for protecting me. You are safe to love and be loved as you are. We are free to let go now. Welcome home.

I finally felt ready to let go of all the proverbial baggage I'd allowed to accumulate for so long. It wasn't mine, which meant I didn't need to carry it any longer. Yet there was a part of me that feared releasing it. I didn't know who I was without it.

If you can relate to any piece of this, maybe you're like me in that you didn't realize you needed permission to finally let that shit go. So in case that's you, here it is, my dear...

Permission to release.

It's time for you to begin living as the *you* that survived... the one worthy of taking up space...the one destined for greatness...the one deserving of all that you desire. You don't have to carry it any longer. It's okay to set it down and move forward without it. Your choice to do so will not change the truth of your experiences. This will not make you less of a warrior. This will not change the fact that you overcame and still continue to show up in your life, even if you know you're not shining as brightly as you're capable of emanating. When you're willing to let it go, know you're supported and that the next chapter in your very own book is waiting to be written—*by you.*

Healing Happens in Letting Go

In talking with fellow survivors, I often see these common themes in one way or another. Over-responsibility, lack of boundaries, over-protectiveness, self-deprecating self-talk, giving away personal power, feeling the need to *earn* love, questioning our worthiness, building walls to keep us safe, carrying baggage from years of pain and sorrow and heartache.

I can see these things because I, too, have experienced many of them firsthand. I have compassion for those still struggling to make sense of it all, doing their best to find purpose in their pain. I also happen to believe with my whole heart that we're all capable of healing these wounds and finding a home to reside in and build from with a brand new foundation. It can often feel easier to just let things be, choosing to remain the same instead of changing at the risk of more loss. But what I've come to understand is that the things we "lose" as we step further into our truth are never really lost because as I've previously mentioned, things (and people) meant to stay long-term don't leave. And the ones that do have served their purpose, so it's best to make peace with the pain and loosen your grip. Instead of expending energy on figuring out *why*, focus on the gratitude for what was, taking that into your next phase of living bravely and wildly *you.*

Please don't confuse this simple explanation as *easy to handle.* Our emotions are often complicated. Let them come, and let them go. Trust that it's all been placed perfectly for your highest and best.

I know for some, hearing this may seem bewildering. There are plenty of people who can, with ease, let things go and move on. However, for people like us (survivors), those who've had our safety shaken, and possibly experienced abandonment and loss of love (which we then internalized as our fault or our identity), permission to release the pain of our experiences can be freeing.

We have dealt with enough already. Holding onto the past, or the pain of others–which many of us experienced first-hand through trauma caused by others' pain–is unnecessary. I understand it's comfortable, and it's what we know. But as I echo throughout this book...*let change change you.* There is so much freedom and power in letting go, in allowing ourselves to soar above the confines of our current reality. It can (and I believe it *should*) feel good to exist in both our inner and outer world. So if there is shit weighing you down, get honest about it and ask yourself...

How long am I willing to carry the weight of this pain?
What would feel better in its place?
Can I give myself the permission I've been seeking (possibly through external circumstances) and finally let it all go?

Our Loss Is Their Loss Too

Understandably, when I'd shared my experience of rape with a stranger of sorts, this truth left him and I both at a loss for words. But instead of trying to fill the uncomfortable silence, I sat with it, letting the heaviness fall from my shoulders, feeling the warmth of my tears catch in the corners of my eyes. This provided an opportunity to create space for a new story to emerge, but that didn't stop the old questions from arising. *Would he leave? Would he see me differently? Would this make me "too broken" to love?*

After a brief period of time had passed, he wrapped me in his arms and soothed me with the words I didn't even know I needed to hear: "I'm so sorry that happened to you." But it wasn't from pity. Suddenly, I could feel the shifting happening on a deep, visceral level. My fear began to dissipate, and instead of speaking, I offered my silence as a way of acknowledging his kindness, a smile finding my lips in place of words unspoken.

So often, loved ones of survivors find themselves paralyzed in silence. *What should I say? How should I act? What should I do? How can I help?* Over the years, after speaking with so many survivors and quite a large group of loved ones trying their best to understand and cope themselves, what I have found to be true is that there is really no right way to be. When horrible things happen, we are typically ill-prepared. Depending on our own experiences, our response or reaction may not feel supportive to the survivor no matter how hard we try to say the "right" thing. Which is why I have found that pausing and asking some simple questions can be an amazing starting point—an opportunity to gauge the readiness of the person sharing to go deeper, as well as our own capacity to hold space for their experience.

Sadly, our loved ones lose in these situations, too. It's important to acknowledge their feelings as we navigate our experience, when the time feels safe to do so. Of course, I encourage survivors to tend to their wounds *first.* But I also encourage you to remember that you don't have to do it alone. Even if you don't have someone close to you that you feel safe to share these things with, there is so much support out there when we're ready to open ourselves up and receive it. Finding a local survivors group in-person or online, or finding a therapist that specializes in assault and/or sexual abuse, is a great first step. The next step I recommend—after we've acknowledged that what happened to us is real, and we cannot take it back—is to do the work to heal so we can be free. God knows we all deserve that.

Here are some statements/questions to consider when you decide to open the dialogue with your loved ones about your experience (or theirs)...

I have something I'd like to share with you. It feels heavy to say out loud so I want to make sure you have the capacity to be with me as I open myself to you. Is now a good time?

Something's been weighing on me and it feels really scary to share. I'm afraid you might see me differently, stop loving me, or leave me (fill this with whatever feels true for you). My words feel shaky right now but I really need to get this off my heart. Can I ask you to listen while I try to put my feelings into words, and we can open the conversation from there?

And always, acknowledge them for bravely holding your story while you share. You could say something as simple as...

Thank you so much for letting me share this with you. I am working really hard to heal the remnants I've been holding onto, and this has been really hard. It means so much that I have a safe space with you to open myself up and know I'm seen and heard through the lens of love.

Guiding The Conversation

I'm willing to bet that on some level we've all been on the receiving end of having no idea what to say in a challenging conversation. But how good does it feel when we're met with compassion regarding our ignorance, and a willingness to help us understand so that we may support, whether it be listening or providing insight?

Give others the same grace you'd hope for in that kind of situation. Speaking about our deepest pain can be sensitive, not only for us but for those kind enough to hold space for our truths to linger.

Instead of shutting down, lashing out, or taking offense to their questioning or inability to grasp what we've shared, pause and get curious. Invite them to ask questions, acknowledging and honoring your own boundaries in the process of sharing more.

I find that most people want to be helpful. However, when faced with an experience we're unfamiliar with, it may be difficult to say the right thing. We can try, but that doesn't always mean we're successful.

Be prepared for the unexpected, and remain unattached to the outcome. Just as we may want their love and support, chances are high that they, too, want to love and support us. In some cases, though, we may need to guide the conversation. Let this be a growth point for yourself, grounding into the practice of asking for what you need and want to feel loved and supported safely.

Something I try really hard to do any time I am sharing something that feels *big* is to ask the other person if they have space to hear my experience and to share in it with me. This has been revolutionary, as it honors everyone involved while respecting boundaries and setting clear expectations. I've also found it helpful to state whether or not I am simply looking to share to get it out, or if I am desiring feedback as well. I've been told time and time again from both friends and clients that this simple practice has really helped them to be better listeners as well. The goal is not to bombard people with our shit. It's to invite people into our truth so they may have a better insight into who we are. Thus, creating deeper connections and ultimately, better relationships.

This could look like: *Hey, I'm dealing with something right now and I could really use your support. Do you have the space for me to share what's coming up for me? I just need someone to witness my experience. I don't actually need any feedback, I just want to be heard.* And if it's true for you you can add: *I am open to loving, honest feedback.*

We've all said the *wrong* thing so remember that before letting someone's response or reaction get under your skin. And if something is said that feels hurtful or unsupportive, offer your heart in the moment, don't let it fester.

This could look like: *Hey, I know when you said (fill in the blank with whatever hurt you) you meant well. But it actually didn't feel good to me. What would have felt more supportive would have been (fill in the blank with what you needed/desired instead). I really appreciate you taking my feelings into consideration, and I deeply appreciate your willingness to be supportive and loving moving forward.*

Or, you could pose a question such as: *What I heard you say was (fill in the blank). Is that what you meant, or would you like to clarify?*

The saying "we teach people how to treat us" is a humbling, yet often true, statement. So don't allow another person's humanness to get in the way of their heart. If their intentions are pure—which, if they're your friend, is likely the case—give them the benefit of the doubt and talk it out with mutual respect.

Can I Be Brave Enough to Speak My Truth?

Think of all the firsts you've had in your life. There are a lot, some easier than others. But you've made it this far, which tells me...you can do pretty much anything.

Speaking up doesn't have to mean sharing your stories (or secrets) publicly. It also doesn't have to mean sharing them with multiple people, either. But I truly believe there is healing power in community, and that we're not meant to do any of this alone. So when you're ready, take a deep breath and let yourself be messy. Allow your heart to pour from your chest as you see fit, and honor your courage as you invite others into your pain. If you've tried this before, and it's ended poorly, it's understandable that you would be apprehensive about giving it another shot. But I promise you, there is someone out there who will listen, who will hold your truth with care. Give yourself the gift of being witnessed and held. All the shit we tend to carry can be heavy. Put it down, love. And let yourself move forward a little lighter.

It's true that your experiences are part of you, but they do not define you. No matter what you've faced, you can absolutely overcome and be better for those experiences. So shine your light and choose to live your life as you see fit, free to rewrite your story at any given moment.

Bravery is within you. Speaking up is only part of the equation, and it often begins with speaking kindly and compassionately with ourselves first. This may take time and practice, as it does for so many of us. Celebrate the moments you allow yourself to open a little wider and be witnessed fully. Courage is a muscle that needs to be worked on a regular basis for a habit to form. Little by little, as your voice gets louder, your courage will grow stronger. You don't have to tell the world all the things that you've been through. You don't actually have to tell anyone anything! But there is a sense of freedom that comes from opening ourselves up to the world in this way, which is why I am encouraging you to be in the practice of standing tall and shining bright as you navigate the journey toward the ultimate prize: inner peace.

Speaking *up* does not have to mean speaking *out.* Navigating the process however feels best for you is perfect. And when the time is right (for you), open. Let yourself be loved fully, as you are.

8

How Do I Trust Again?

"Nothing ever goes away until it has taught us what we need to know. Nothing ever really attacks us except our own confusion. Perhaps there is no solid obstacle except our own need to protect ourselves from being touched. If we run a hundred miles an hour to the other end of the continent in order to get away from the obstacle, we find the very same problem waiting for us when we arrive. It just keeps returning with new names, forms, manifestations until we learn whatever it has to teach us about where we are separating ourselves from reality, how we are pulling back instead of opening up, closing down instead of allowing ourselves to experience fully whatever we encounter, without hesitating or retreating into ourselves." – Pema Chödrön

For years after my assault, I felt paralyzed, moving through life in a daze with one moment blending into the next. My entire world as I knew it had been turned upside down, leaving me feeling like a shell of a person. And yet,

I held onto whatever remnants were left, no matter how painful it was to keep grasping for the past.

I refused to give up my old identity, as I felt my true essence slipping away. I wrapped my arms around the labels I'd created—*unlovable, unworthy, damaged*—and coaxed myself into believing that to be strong meant to keep going, to push through, to try to forget about the pain. I lied to myself as a way to self-protect in hopes that when I did finally come up for air, I would realize that it was nothing but a bad dream.

Of course, that didn't happen. Because it was real. My story was true, and it was *mine*. Living with it, however, felt harder than masking it. I fought against myself in an effort to hide my shadows by illuminating the highlight reel of my existence, failing to admit that it was a bunch of bullshit; smoke and mirrors acting as saviors to my otherwise chaotic inner world.

To be free of the pain, I needed to befriend it. I needed to find a way to honor what I'd been through, and to learn to trust my body again. I had to mourn the girl who had been stripped of her innocence, and welcome the woman who took her place with open arms...and an open heart.

This would prove to be a more difficult path to walk than I'd imagined. Not because I was angry at myself, or felt any sense of guilt about what had happened. But because doing all of these things would mean I would have to face the grief I was stuffing down inside, admitting that I had no control over what had happened. For someone who grasped for control like a lifeline from a very early age to feel safe, releasing it felt nauseating. Not to mention incredibly scary and uncomfortable.

I would come to realize many years later, after experiencing *twelve* back-to-back losses within the span of two short years, that it is in the space between grief and reflection that we find the silver lining. After my assault, choosing to be with my feelings instead of pushing past them was a muscle I had yet to strengthen. It took a lot of practice (and patience) to accept that vulnerability, both with myself and with others, was necessary if I truly wanted to heal.

As time passed, and I allowed myself to really be with the pain and all that came with it, I was able to hear my heart speak tenderly to my emerging Self. This time, however, I didn't silence her. Instead, I listened, and I vowed to be present for both the pain and the pleasure that this human experience would no doubt provide. I closed my eyes and exhaled deeply as her words...*my words*...pulsated through my body. I felt my sweet Nana holding me, and it was at that moment that I knew I was going to be okay.

Dear one, it's the memories of yesterday that will provide solace as we step into a new day with hope, knowing that each moment we have a choice to embrace the now and be grateful for what was and what will be. The heart will heal. The absence of the old (Self) will seem less as time goes on. The sadness will eventually turn to joy as we remember that, with each experience, we are being asked to open, over and over again. Just as we rise each morning to greet the sun, may you always remember that each breath is a blessing, and each soul we encounter is such a gift... even the people who have caused us pain. The truth remains: we are still here, which means together we have a responsibility to show up and share ourselves with the world. Take that seriously. And smile a little bigger knowing you've still got work to do.

I felt a sense of hope wash over me. I believed those words and wanted to embody them deeply. However, as much as I wanted to believe that peace and healing were possible for me, even after everything I'd endured, my pesky old inner voice of doubt liked to show up and question if it could really be that simple?

Shutting Out Silence

I spent the greater part of college riddled with insomnia, keeping a bottle of NyQuil on my nightstand as a crutch. I was facing so much physical pain without answers, that I felt like the only thing I had any control over was my mind. Funny how years later I would realize that, trauma or not, that's precisely the point. Our mind is a garden, and our thoughts can either be weeds or they can become glorious flowers with our tender love and care. We have to decide how we want our garden to look and take the actions necessary to align ourselves to achieving that outcome.

I heard my grandmother's voice in my head regularly, "This too shall pass, little one." As much as I knew that to be true deep down, there was a large part of me that wished my trauma had never happened in the first place. I moved through the motions, but I parked my *e-motions* on the doorstep, where they sat and waited for an invitation inside. Feeling them seemed too big. I was afraid that if I let them in, I'd never get out alive...and the fear and lack of control would consume me.

I used my days to preoccupy myself with friends, school, and work. But the nights haunted me like a monster hiding under my bed. The darkness would come, as would the silence, and once again I was left alone with my thoughts. All the mental buzzing kept me on high alert, and the only way I knew to shut off the noise was to take a dose of NyQuil and disappear into the wee hours of the night, hoping to get at least a few hours of peace and quiet before doing it all over again.

I was completely overwhelmed and prayed every night for things to *be easy*. Until I learned what I needed to learn, this routine played on repeat like a broken record. At the time, I couldn't understand why I kept experiencing the same shit, like it was Groundhog Day every day, and I couldn't stop the madness. Looking back, it's so obvious that I was unconsciously holding onto victimhood, albeit silently, in order to make sense of something that, at the time, made no sense at all. This lasted throughout my twenties as a way to numb and dissociate, until I found my way *through* and stopped chasing the proverbial rainbow that I imagined existed on the other side of the pain.

When I went back to school to study holistic health and nutrition, after spending over a decade in self-study and self-experimentation with all sorts of herbs, "potions," and tinctures, my insomnia had lessened, but it refused to leave me completely. Sleep, as it turns out, was one of my triggers. I couldn't help but wonder if someone would sneak into my room while I was unconscious and violate me all over again. There was safety in being awake, or at least somewhat conscious. The darkness was where monsters preyed on their victims, after all, and I refused to be a victim ever again.

Learning to Trust Myself

After experiencing any sort of trauma, it makes sense that we would question ourselves, namely our intuition. After all, we made the choice to do the thing (for me, that meant saying yes to a seemingly innocent date), and look what happened! How could we possibly believe ourselves after that, when we've proven we're untrustworthy?

For me, my entire body screamed *"NO!"* when my rapist initially asked me out. And while I listened and honored that "no" for months, eventually his persistence annoyed me enough to change my mind. That decision, a slap in the face to my intuition, was obviously a very monumental choice point for me. It communicated to my parts (as they're referred to in Internal Family Systems or IFS) that they were not in charge, and I was going to do whatever the hell I wanted, regardless of their best efforts to keep me safe.

I was so focused on getting this arrogant dude off my back that I blatantly ignored the little voice inside telling me with conviction that saying "yes" to his invitation was not a good idea. I made a choice, which inevitably had consequences that I could not have fathomed to be even remotely possible. But that *did not* make what happened my fault *because of that choice*.

We all have an inner voice, and when we listen to this whisper, it can be a powerful guide. Our inner voice is our intuitive knowing—quiet but powerful—put in place to protect us and pave a clear path to our deepest truth. Ignoring it, however, often provides the shadow side of alignment (*misalignment*), leaving us vulnerable to the unknown. Sometimes, the thought of the unknown feels so exciting that chasing the high is enough for us to gladly ignore that inner voice. As a rule-breaker myself, I understand wanting to test the waters of these decisions. However, there is a difference between *going against the grain* and choosing to step outside the lines to prove a point or gain another perspective, versus *ignoring the blaring signs* for safety. It's up to us to learn to distinguish between these intuitive feelings, so we can move closer to the pleasure we crave, instead of unknowingly inviting danger into our experience.

It would take me a really long time to trust myself again. I began to self-sabotage through relationships, and found myself holding onto toxic people, which in retrospect I believe was a form of self-punishment. I was disappointed in myself for ignoring the red flags in the past (saying yes when I wanted to say no). So now, instead of ignoring the red flags, I was *choosing* them (by way of horrible partners), hoping for a different outcome as a way to justify that not all red flags were bad...which only harmed me in the long run.

I was brilliant at covering up my self-destructive behavior. I went about my days as if nothing had happened, filling every ounce of empty space with distraction. Soon after my assault, I met a man whom I spent three-and-a-half years in a relationship with—a man who continuously cheated on me, even getting someone else pregnant while we were together. It was during this relationship that I found myself in a major shame cycle. I justified my choice to stay with him with the belief that I was lucky! I was the damaged one, and he still wanted to be with me, so it made sense that I would endure his infidelity because I believed that it was what I deserved. Deep down, though, I knew the lies I was feeding myself were a crock of shit. I *knew* I deserved better, but for some reason, I wouldn't let myself *have* better.

He never knew my secret. And when I finally found the courage to leave him for good, I knew in my bones that my life was about to take a serious turn.

That dysfunctional relationship changed me. It took me into the lowest lows and showed me the depths of my pain in ways I hadn't been willing to face previously. And even though I was still hiding, I began to feel my soul coming back to life, whispering love notes to my heart in the empty spaces I had kept closed for so long. I could feel the shifting happening, making room so I could fill those once empty spaces with my truth and eventually...more love.

Learning to trust myself has been a continuous practice since the night of my assault. Even to this day, I still have moments when I question myself and my decisions, despite feeling the answer deep within that I did nothing wrong. There are times I want to choose outside the lines, knowing that any choice other than the "right" one for me will inevitably bring pain, yet I toy with the idea anyway. Maybe it's the little rebel on my shoulder begging to play, or possibly my ego testing my commitment to move on. Whatever the reason, I've learned over time that only I know what's truly best for me. So, for me, making aligned decisions often requires space for silence and solitude.

Sometimes, tuning in and feeling into my intuition brings up a lot of emotions. Fear arises, and I can feel the panic revving up my nervous system as I ask myself, *What if I make the wrong decision again?* At times, anxiety finds me and I'm paralyzed by indecision. Yet I've learned that feeling stuck is okay, too. When I take the space I need to feel into my heart and inner knowing, there is inevitably a sense of peace that comes. That's when I know I've hit my sweet spot, and the right decision shows up for my choosing. But I must be present enough to the moment at hand to recognize what's being offered. Maybe you can relate to this.

We've all made decisions at some point that we look back on with regret, or judgment, or curiosity about what might have been different if only we had...(insert: a different choice). The key isn't to *not* question ourselves, the key is to learn from our experiences and commit to coming back to our truth when we're faced with the opportunity to choose again.

If you're a people-pleaser, recovering or otherwise, it may support you to ask yourself a series of questions when making decisions as a way to sharpen your trust muscle. I've found that getting quiet, and feeling into the body, naming the sensations and where they're felt, is a powerful way to find your truest self again.

Then ask yourself:

Once I've made my decision, how do I want to feel?
Does this decision bring me closer to or farther away from my desired state (peace, joy, etc.)?
Would choosing something different feel better, more aligned?
What am I afraid will happen if I make the "wrong" decision?
Am I willing to bet on myself and lean into self-trust in this moment as a practice to gain the confidence I crave for my decisions moving forward?

Then act accordingly. Trust is earned. That includes the trust we have with ourselves. Just as with a loved one, when *we* break that trust, it's up to *us* to repair it. And to do so takes intentional action, compassion, and a whole lotta love.

Be gentle with yourself and your process. Remember that it's yours, and how you choose to repair it is in your hands (and heart).

Body Signals

There are so many facets of healing to be addressed after assault, or any type of violation of Self. Intimacy, for instance, is quite interesting. Fortunately, I did not experience any lingering fears around physical touch afterward, but I know many people who have. I will say, however, that I became much more in tune with my body after the event, as I learned how to re-engage with my senses and discover what safety meant for me now, given all I had been through.

I became hyper-aware of my surroundings—constantly looking over my shoulder, jumping at the slightest noise or movement. This response has followed me through my healing, although it's become much quieter. Now, I can laugh when I am easily startled whereas previously, I would feel a wave of panic wash over me as my nervous system went into high alert, my palms began to sweat and my breath became shallow—and I would freeze. It's taken time and patience to get to this place, which is far from perfect, but it's progress. For me, that's enough.

After the rape, I no longer looked at strangers the same way. Once an openly trusting person, although typically aware and discerning, I instantly felt tension in my body when placed in a crowd or unfamiliar environment. I felt like everyone knew my secret (although at the time, nobody did), and they were all looking at me. At first, I judged these feelings and the heightened sensitivity I had to life. I wanted to forget about what had happened, to move forward without having to work so hard to simply exist. Life felt overly complicated all of a sudden, and it soon became exhausting.

This was the point in my journey where I surrendered, vowing to become besties with my intuition. I'd always had a good sense of people, although I didn't always follow my gut. But now those fluttery feelings I'd once struggled to understand were on steroids, and they could not be ignored any longer.

I felt like my body was a lightbulb and my intuition was the switch. I would meet someone, or walk into a new environment, and instantly there would be a zing of energy pulsing through my body. So, I got in the habit of asking my body for guidance when I felt unsure on the surface and over time, I began to learn the power of sensation as a signal to *respond or react.*

If my throat became tense, *what was I afraid to say?* If my shoulders stiffened, *what was I trying to hold the weight of (and could I release it)?* I became very attuned to bullshit, sniffing it out like a K9 on duty. To this day, I can meet someone and they don't have to say a word, I can simply feel their energy and know whether or not they're someone I want to be around. And I trust that, without explanation. Because this sixth sense has never let me down.

When it comes to romantic relationships and intimacy, there were things I didn't realize would be triggering until I experienced them. Like feeling hands touching my neck, even playfully. I don't like it—it triggers the fuck outta me—and healing or not, it's a hard *no* for me! While some survivors find themselves giving their bodies away freely after sexual trauma, I saw my body as even more sacred afterward. It was my temple, and although I couldn't stop my rapist on the night of my assault, I would never allow anyone to take advantage of me or my body ever again.

I didn't have a problem saying no—and because I was flirtatious, some guys labeled me a "tease" when my playful demeanor didn't match my unwillingness to get naked and sleep with them. At times, I wondered if I was doing something wrong. Was I being an asshole or a prude or leading them on? Yet I knew better, and I was none of those things. I was simply doing my best to feel safe while also allowing myself to experience and explore different aspects of my desires as a sexual being who had, unfortunately, been violated against my will. I was navigating my boundaries, as much as these men were pushing their own. More often than not, this subtle tension resulted in frustration on both our parts.

As I became more confident in myself, my body confidence followed. I practiced gratitude, thanking my body for how strong she was and how hard she worked to keep me safe. I still had moments of anger, especially during the many years struggling with illness and hospitalizations, but I always made sure to praise her for her efforts. I found that the more I tuned in, turned inward, and honored her signals, the more deeply connected we became and the easier it felt to make empowered decisions for my healing and overall happiness. She didn't choose to be raped, *she was forced.* And from that experience, I saw it as my responsibility to protect her even more so, and show her how to love herself, regardless of her past.

Our body is always speaking to us. Are you listening? More importantly, are you honoring what she's telling you? I promise, this practice will not only help you in your own healing process, but it will magnetize the same vibrational energy and caliber of people that come into your experience, making attunement and alignment with safety, joy, and ease that much easier.

Think of a time when you remember feeling an *inner sensation* (physical) pertaining to your *outer surroundings.* Maybe it was walking alone at night, feeling the hair on your body stand up straight as you rounded an unknown corner. Or getting on a roller coaster and feeling the fear move from your head to your stomach, as the ride whipped you from side to side, up and down.

This is known as *interoception*, which can be conscious or unconscious. Interoception happens when we become aware of the felt sensations within our body, including the function of our internal organs (think: *heart beat, breath, hunger, emotions*). During interoception, the brain is able to integrate the signals occurring in its different regions (like the thalamus, brainstem, etc.) with felt bodily sensations to form our perception of the experience.

In the moment, you felt the sensations based on your environment. You were tapped into your body—and that is the goal as we move through this messy, unpredictable world. For many, conscious interoception takes a lot of work to master. We tend to move so quickly through the world, often on autopilot, neglecting to take the time to feel what we feel in our body at any given moment. This creates a sort of disconnection with ourselves, and for many survivors, learning to come back to our bodies after trauma can feel incredibly scary and alarming. For many of us, we've spent so much time dissociating from our physical body, the thought of connecting the pieces again may seem foreign, even strange. But this integration is crucial if we want to truly embody our healing, to know what it feels like to be whole in our bodies again.

Take a minute and name the feeling or sensation you can recall in your own experience based on the examples I provided above. Then name the place in your body where you felt it. How did you move through the sensation? How did you feel afterward?

Power in the Pain

Like I did when stepping into my first romantic relationship after my assault, many others I've spoken with have also fallen into the trap of feeling *deserving of less* because of their experience(s) with trauma.

Let me just say, it's total bullshit. You deserve all the things your heart desires, period. Full stop.

No matter what you've been through, none of it defines the beauty that is you. You are enough and deserving because you exist, and for no other reason. And pain, whether self-inflicted or not, is *not* a barrier to your worth.

You don't need to accept *less* because you feel *less than deserving*. Instead, use the energy you're expending on making excuses for others (while tolerating their mediocre or downright destructive behavior) to be with yourself and heal. You have the ability to turn your pain into power. You, dear one, are the answer you're seeking.

When my ex-boyfriend was cheating, I knew better than to remain in the relationship. I actually had proof it was happening, yet I stayed. Why? Because I wanted someone to want me, even if he totally sucked. That belief had everything to do with me and my perception of my worth, which was clearly low at the time. I accepted the pain of that relationship hoping it would lead to the pleasure I desired. Instead, staying with him only led to more pain. I held on so tightly because all I kept thinking was, *Who will want me...this damaged and broken shell of a woman?* I was berating myself for things that happened which were outside of my control. It was that same low-vibrational thinking that brought in a low-vibrational match (in the form of a douchebag), which ultimately served as a beautiful teacher revealing all the things I *didn't* want in a partner.

Only I could *choose into* and *out of* that experience. Yes, it took me three-and-a-half years to find the courage and self-respect to leave. But it was exactly the time I needed to come to the conclusion that I *could* have better and I *wasn't* broken, which kinda sounds crazy to me now. There was a ton of heartache during that period in my life, but because of the heartache a lot of healing took place. For that, I am grateful.

Pleasure is available to you, in all the ways. You do not need to sacrifice your dreams and desires for one second longer. More often than not, your pain, while unfortunate, has purpose. At the very least, your pain offers lessons to take away and use moving forward. So accept the hand you've been dealt, and then create your own version of a royal flush! Stop blaming your current reality on past circumstances because guess what? They've happened, and nothing you say or do can change that. The good news is, you absolutely have control over how you choose to respond. And *that* is real power.

Finding Pleasure

I mentioned intimacy, and I want to dive into that a bit more because I truly believe that passion, sex and physical connection have their own place in healing, too. If you have experienced some kind of sexual trauma, moving safely into sex and intimacy with yourself or another may feel triggering. Don't force it. Be aware of what's coming up for you in these instances so you can actively work to target those triggers, to find your way out of the pain and safely into pleasure.

Here are some questions to consider regarding intimacy, which does not necessarily mean sex...

What are some ways you can support yourself to feel more empowered?
What are some coping skills that have worked well for you?
What can you put in place to help you remember to use these skills as needed?
What positive qualities did you develop in response to managing a traumatic life event, possibly in which you didn't choose to participate but happened to you anyway?
How can these skills help you in the present and future?

I can't recall the first time I had sex after being raped. But I know it took some time for me to feel comfortable *receiving* pleasure for many years afterwards. I had created a story that accepting kindness from others (including pleasure) meant it could also be taken away or taken advantage of; instead, I was better off *giving* as much as possible to keep them close and keep my guard up. That way, I could choose *out of* the pain if I saw it coming without being too emotionally attached.

I dove head first into the study of sexuality and tantra. For years, I read everything I could get my hands on to better understand how to empower myself and safely move into receiving without shame or guilt. I began a healthy and intentional self-pleasure practice, exploring my body as a way to discover what felt good. Although, more importantly, to me it was about connecting deeply to what felt *safe.* I thought that if I could learn to touch my body without wincing or feeling wrong or bad when things felt good, eventually that would translate into my romantic relationships. Turns out, I was right!

I got really curious about what I liked and didn't like. I teased all my senses, playing with taste, touch, scent, sound, and sight. I later learned about the Erotic Blueprint™ created by Miss Jaiya, which helped me better understand my sensitivity to my environment—not only my desire to connect my mind, body and soul during my sexual encounters, but my *need* to have all of these factors in place to feel safe and connected to myself and my partner. I became highly attuned to my body and its signals, desiring to experience pleasure at the highest level without apology or feeling the need to explain myself. I was a sexual being re-learning how to have a healthy relationship with my body, while embracing my growing sexual appetite. I had nothing to be ashamed of, and I refused to hide it or apologize for it.

At that point, I'd never really heard anyone talk about self-pleasure (masturbation) so this was a whole new world to me. I'd always been curious about sex, and felt comfortable openly talking about it with friends, but I'd never allowed myself the freedom to experience what I was choosing to step into now. I was filled with excitement...and hope! I could feel the healing taking place as my body learned to relax and settle into the invitations I presented through pleasure and play. I would close my eyes and start from my head all the way down to my toes asking, *Body, what do you need right now? Body, how do you feel right now? Body, where do you want to be touched right now, and how?* Then I honored her. In turn, she honored me back.

We don't need to wait for another person to show up to experience pleasure. In fact, I find that when we grant ourselves permission to explore and experience our deepest desires with ourselves first, it translates beautifully when we are met by another safe person willing and ready to share this kind of connection with us. Imagine the most delicious bodily sensation you can possibly fathom. Now imagine sharing that with someone you love deeply, who values, honors, respects and appreciates you. The pleasure available is like nothing else. But you've gotta allow yourself to surrender to your primal senses to receive the pleasure waiting for you.

Here are some questions to consider as you explore your own sexuality and capacity for intimacy...

Where on/in your body can you touch and, in turn, feel positive sensations?
What are you still not allowing yourself to experience?
What do you need to release to feel safe in your body and during sexual encounters, both with self and partnered?
What is working well for you in terms of healing your relationship with your body?
If partnered, what fears/desires do you want to share with them to create a deeper connection?
What are your fears in doing so?
Are you willing to release these fears, and re-commit to your sexual liberation/freedom?
If not, why?

Do yourself a favor and do whatever you've gotta do to get to a place where experiencing pleasure is possible for you. It's been my experience that once you step foot into this level of euphoria, there's no turning back. And whether with yourself or another, there's healing available in your sexual expansion. Let it happen.

Your Boundaries Don't Need an Explanation

As you learn to trust yourself on a deeper level, you'll likely begin to see where you've watered down your boundaries for one reason or another. So often we tag some sort of reasoning to the end of our *no's*, which I think, from a biological standpoint, goes back to the human condition and our desire to be accepted. The truth is, you don't owe anyone anything, especially when it comes to the boundaries you've set for yourself. "No" is a complete sentence. So please stop apologizing or trying to make others understand your decisions.

Thinking about this now, I can't help but laugh. I was the worst when it came to asking my mom, *"Why?...But, why?...Why, though?"* All the time! No wonder she'd get frustrated and respond with an agitated, *"BECAUSE I SAID SO!"* Sure, some things were just straight up annoying and I was probably being a brat. But other things, pertaining to her boundaries, didn't need an explanation. She'd chosen those boundaries for herself and the *why* was really none of my business.

The truth is, it's nobody's business why you've created the boundaries you have. What matters is the intention behind doing so, and honoring those intentions fully with confidence. However, to avoid any confusion, there's a big difference between *walls* and boundaries.

Walls keep people out and are usually created from past pain, trauma, and uncomfortable experiences.

Boundaries honor the highest expression of your truth and are established based on self-love, self-respect, and knowing your intimate needs, wants, and beliefs as to what feels best for you. These, too, often come from personal experiences. The difference?

Walls repel.
Boundaries attract.

Walls say, *I'm afraid of feeling (insert shitty emotion) again so I'm going to protect myself by closing myself to the possibility that things can be different this time around.*

Boundaries say, *I've learned from previous experiences what will and will not work for me and because of this, I'm clear what I'm willing to allow and accept in my experience as a way to love myself deeper and create better feeling experiences moving forward.*

I understand that walls often help us to feel safe in the moment; nobody wants to relive shitty emotions. But what if the very things you want to avoid feeling are also the very things to bring you closer to the truth of who you are and what you came here to learn and grow through in this lifetime? Not to mention, the opportunities that staying open brings when you create solid boundaries that invite in more of the *yes* and allow you to clearly see the *no's* for what they are...*noise!*

I believe that every experience we have is meant to teach us something. The *what* is up for interpretation.

When we choose to see the past through the eyes of love, fear dissipates and it becomes easier to follow the breadcrumbs back home to that inner knowing we've all got lingering within. We're not here to keep people out. We're here to figure out who has earned the right to stay, and open ourselves up to more love, belonging, and becoming in the process.

In my Somatic Trauma Therapy Certification training, one of our instructors, Staci K. Haines, author of *The Politics of Trauma: Somatics, Healing and Social Justice*, shared this consent practice with us, and I wanted to pass it along to you in case it supports you on your journey as well.

In any given situation, you have agency to say a *centered yes, centered maybe,* or *centered no* based on what's important to you instead of deferring to an automatic response based on conditioning or past experiences/responses. Use this exercise to establish boundaries that feel aligned in your body.

1. Seated or standing, relax your jaw, your eyeballs, your shoulders and all your limbs.
2. Let your breath relax all the way down your spine.
3. Choose a person or situation that you want to practice boundaries with (this is imperative for this exercise).
4. Notice your body sensations: temperature, any pressure, tightness, etc.
5. Place one foot in front of the other, then extend your arms out straight in front of you (this is a "no"). Now place your arms in front of you, with your hands below waist, palms down (this is a "maybe"). Now place your legs side-by-side, with your palms up, and your arms down at a diagonal by your side (this is a "yes").
6. How does each position feel in your body? Be honest with yourself.

This practice allows for *choice* vs. jumping into a reactive response, and may support you as you navigate your own boundaries with a new sense of confidence.

How Do I Trust Again?

We can only begin to trust others and the world around us by first learning to trust ourselves above all else. Boundaries are a great starting point as we learn to navigate what feels true asking questions like, *What does my intuition say?* Then, we can start to reclaim and relearn how to use *"no"* in an empowered way.

You may be someone who has a default yes or no. Pay attention to this. Avoid judgment—instead, be in the practice of curiosity and awareness. If you lean one way or another, feel into why this is. Did you have a past experience that led you to believe that either/or was better or safer to choose? Do you still feel that's true now?

Trauma is *caused by* experiences, but trauma itself *causes* a "fixed reactive state" within our bodies (parts) that becomes non-responsive to current circumstances (your reality right now). Traumatic experiences break apart some of our core human needs: *safety, belonging, and dignity*. Healing brings these core needs back together. If we become stuck in what *has happened* instead of *what's currently happening*, it can be confusing to sort out the best course of action to take, including conscious decision making and healthy boundary setting.

By stepping out of a fixed reactive state, through healing and practice, we can come back to the present moment and choose what feels true for us in the here and now. Confidence is born through action. To gain more confidence and begin really trusting ourselves, we've gotta take a leap of faith, building our wings on the way down.

Trust is a muscle, and it's honed through experienced outcomes. So allow yourself the opportunity to prove to yourself that you can make decisions that support your highest and best. You will mess up (because you're human). But I'm willing to bet that you'll also make yourself proud in the process, which will only increase your level of trust in yourself and, eventually, your ability and willingness to trust others as well.

9

Will I Ever Feel Safe to Let Love In?

"Things are always in transition, if we could only realize it. Nothing ever sums itself up in the way that we like to dream about. The off-center, in-between state is an ideal situation, a situation in which we don't get caught and we can open our hearts and minds beyond limit. It's a very tender, nonaggressive, open-ended state of affairs. To stay with that shakiness—to stay with a broken heart, with a rumbling stomach, with the feeling of hopelessness and wanting to get revenge—that is the path of true awakening. Sticking with that uncertainty, getting the knack of relaxing in the midst of chaos, learning not to panic—this is the spiritual path." – Pema Chödrön, When Things Fall Apart

The emotions that come after trauma are valid, real, and deeply personal. The questions we ask ourselves on the path to healing often come from societal programming and self-imposed limitations ("this happened so I must be bad, wrong, damaged, broken…"), as well as the stories we've told ourselves based on who we think we *should* be, or how we think we *should* act. Whether it's right or wrong is irrelevant. The fact remains, when we experience something that shakes us to our core, we will never be the same. There is inevitably an element of healing required to feel safe and whole again.

You've likely seen, heard, or personally experienced the effects of attempting to have a healthy relationship post-trauma without doing the work necessary to heal the wounds before stepping into partnership. More often than not, this is a recipe for heartache. Not because there's anything wrong with us (or them), but because relationships are living, breathing things, and they require our active (and conscious) participation to thrive. They need to be nurtured the same way you manage a bank account—there are deposits and withdrawals, a healthy balance of what's needed to keep you alive and safe. If we don't have the capacity to show up fully for ourselves, which is what healing provides, then it becomes impossible for us to show up fully for the relationships we seek. This makes love at its deepest level, both given and received, that much harder to obtain and support.

In my experience, those who jump into relationships before they're really ready have a much harder time allowing themselves the space necessary for deep healing to take place. Not because they don't desire it, but because they have instead chosen to fill the space where pain once lived with a better feeling (i.e. lust/love, partnership). Totally unstandable. The problem is, more often than not, this type of relationship is unsustainable. And the pain of the loss of the relationship only adds to the pain of the unresolved trauma that's been suppressed and neglected, making the climb upward feel that much more daunting.

Trauma as a Tool for Transformation

Instead of tucking our traumas away, this is an invitation to open ourselves to healing. While I don't wish my experience upon anyone, I can honestly say that it served as my greatest and most impactful teacher, for which I will forever be grateful. That one single night changed the trajectory of my entire life and opened me up to a completely different way of thinking and being in the world. It was hard to manage, especially while silent. Yet in my struggle I found my strength, and it's where my transformation from girl into woman began. Never in my wildest dreams would I have imagined this being part of my story, but the fact that it happened showed me that I was capable of far more than I realized.

If you allow change to change you, it can and it will. Be intentional in your choosing, however, as *change* wears many faces. It's easy to want to remain angry, or keep your guard up to keep people out. It can feel much harder to release the negative emotions and choose feelings that seem counterintuitive to your negative experience because they're unfamiliar, which can be scary. The gift of trauma is that it opens us up to transformation in ways that far exceed our logical mind and asks us to evolve at a rate that we may not have been ready for. It's a journey that only other survivors can truly understand, and it can be really beautiful...as well as challenging and confusing.

Loving What Is

I'll never forget looking at myself in the mirror after my assault, mascara streaked down my face, befuddled by my reflection. *Who was this person staring back at me with empty eyes?* Weeks went by, and each time I looked in the mirror, the same question plagued me. I wasn't sure I would ever be able to look at myself the same way again, which made sense given that I was *not* the same person I'd been before that transformative night.

I wish I could say I bounced back quickly and was able to move on and begin loving myself easily. But that wasn't the case. Instead I struggled silently for years, hoping to find a sense of home, any semblance of familiarity, really. The problem, however, was that I was unconsciously seeking love outside of myself, instead of working to build a new home for love within myself first.

Looking back, I can see how desperate I was to fit in, to forget what had happened. While I never attempted to water down my personality or passion for life, I certainly kept this enormous piece of my story a secret hoping I would be seen as *normal*, like everyone else. Perception is funny, though, since it's clear that there is no such thing as "normal" and chasing the idea of "fitting in" is a complete waste of time and energy.

We (all of us) were born to stand out! To shine, set an example, and be who we are in all our strange, different, weird and wild glory! Yet we spend so much of our days observing others and placing labels on the right or wrong way to be. I wish I could go back and tell my 19-year-old self that she was beautiful and enough, *in spite of* her experiences, and no amount of withholding or self-abuse would ever change that.

I talk a lot about self-love, but for those of us who have been beaten down, literally or figuratively, it can be a foreign concept we only pretend to grasp. We might think that *buying* our way home to ourselves with *things* will solve the problem when, in fact, it only adds to the noise, taking us further away from our desire to feel safe, settled, and free in our mind and body.

Unconditional and absolute self-love has nothing to do with anything outside of ourselves. Yet I have found that for many of us on our healing path, we use *shiny objects* as distractions, even giving ourselves to random people in hopes of feeling desired, to feel better about ourselves and our circumstances. Far too often, instead of filling us up, they become more of a distraction from the Self, which maybe we are just too afraid to face. Don't get me wrong, indulging in nice things and experiences that feel delicious are amazing and I advocate for them fully! But they are not the solution to self-love because self-love, at its core, is an inside job.

If you notice yourself seeking "love" outside of yourself, ask yourself:

What am I hiding from?
Why is the idea of disconnecting from the external world to be with myself in silence/stillness so uncomfortable?
Who am I without all of the noise (distraction)?
Am I willing to get quiet enough to listen and honor what I truly need and want?

It's time to let go of all the *doing* so the *love* we seek has room to show up.

I've spent so much time in the *doing* mentality. I have burned out, broken down, beaten myself up for not being further along in my life, for not making an impact at the caliber I feel called to create, for not already having it "all figured out." I have repeated this cycle more than once, and each time I think I've finally gotten to the other side, I realize there's always another side to where we end up...

The journey never actually stops, it simply changes.
We change.

What if the level of *love* our soul craves is simply the awareness of the love we are failing to *give* to ourselves? I invite you to sit with that for a moment.

When we tap into our hearts and come home to our truth, what comes up may be hard to face. When we accept that we are attracting what we *are*, it can be humbling and frustrating. It can also be liberating, and an invitation for us to move away from the noise and tap into the places within that feel scary and uncertain.

The experience of be-ing human is complex, yet when we allow ourselves the gift of acceptance of what is—within and around us—I believe we also allow ourselves to tap further into love of Self and others.

And isn't love (connection) the ultimate goal?

Stop the Self-Sabotage Cycle

It's my deep belief that most of us are walking around craving connection. We seek to fill that space, yet we have no idea what it actually means *to connect*, which leads us down the path of unhealthy distractions, some of which I previously mentioned.

We question why we feel alone when we're surrounded by so much noise (like social media), and I believe that's our answer: *noise.*

We've mistaken distraction for connection, leaving us unsatisfied and craving more, like an addict looking for a fix. Instead of feeling our truth, we stuff our fears, hiding behind our screens and staying "busy." We're subconsciously choosing *disconnection* as a way to protect ourselves from taking risks that might leave us in pain. On the flip side, these risks may very well be what bring us more joy than we could fathom, but that means getting uncomfortable long enough to find out.

We want to experience the presence of connected love, but we've yet to understand and accept that it starts with our willingness to first love ourselves.

Love is a daily choice, whether we're loving ourselves or others. How far we're willing to go to experience what's available is ultimately up to us. Are you setting standards for what feels good and true, or are you building walls out of fear? When you're willing to look in the mirror and accept your role in your loneliness and take action to heal, we all win.

Love always wins.

Settling for Crumbs

The saying *we attract what we are* holds some merit here. While this does not necessarily mean that if you're attracting assholes you must be an asshole, although maybe. It does, however, mean that if you're attracting things and people that feel out of alignment with your true desires, there's likely something to look at within in order to effectively change that pattern (the story you're telling yourself about what you deserve, or lack thereof, being one of them).

So many survivors carry a false belief that we should just *be happy with what we get* when it comes to accepting *less than* mind-blowing love. I know because I used to be one of them. As if, because we've been through something horrible, all we deserve are horrible things. But that terrible event(s) didn't make *us* terrible people. I would argue it's quite the opposite! So why do so many of us walk around settling for crumbs, instead of demanding the whole damn meal...or a seat at the head of the table?

I believe this lack of worthiness stems from a disconnection to our authentic Self, and our inability or unwillingness to let go of the past so we can fully step into the life meant for us in the present moment.

When we learn to connect with who we are now, versus defining ourselves by what happened to us in the past, we begin to confidently stand in our worth and stop settling for bullshit. Only then can we see the limitless opportunities available to us. Reconnection can feel uncomfortable, even impossible, at first. But trust me when I say, it is absolutely possible and you are worth the effort it takes to become a master at this.

A renowned addiction expert, speaker and author, Dr. Gabor Maté holds expertise in trauma, addiction, stress and childhood development. He talks often about *compassionate inquiry* which, despite the term, does not allow much room for story.

Instead of getting stuck in the past, part of our work is to recognize the past only for its role in our present experience. Otherwise, our past is really not that important. *Compassionate inquiry* is about getting to the root of the issues we're still holding onto, and then being safely and consciously guided back to our truth. The end result? Reconnection to the Self.

We come into this world connected to ourselves. It's only through our lived experiences that we begin to disconnect, which creates our suffering. Authenticity shows up by clearing away the rubble we still carry from our past—including old thought patterns, stories, and feelings—and making room for the truth of the present moment to be fully seen and experienced.

There is a dance that happens as we stretch ourselves into our truth. Within this dance is a part of us that will ask us to remain the same, stay put, "don't change," simply to appease our ego's desire for safety.

It's beautiful, really, that our subconscious parts care so much about our well-being. But just as we, the conscious soul living in the here and now, have no idea what's next, neither does our ego. And this is the point in the dance where I love to focus on gratitude, reminding myself that I am safe to trust my next step.

Who we are in this moment is not who we will ultimately become. While that can feel exciting, maybe even a little frightening (the great unknown), what a beautiful reminder to be present and give thanks for the person who has come this far. Instead of worrying, focus instead on gratitude for the version of ourselves looking back at us in the mirror, possibly a little older, wiser...maybe a bit more fucked up. The complexities of this human experience are here to be celebrated. And who we are, including our dreams for our future self, deserve to be acknowledged and honored.

My invitation to you is to commit to your joy, your desires, your dreams, your stretchy goals. Drop the notion that you "should" be anything but yourself, exactly who and where you are right now. Because who you are, and who you will become, is ever-evolving. No matter what you've been led to believe, you are worthy of all that you can imagine... and so much more.

Love Thyself

It wasn't that long ago when I found myself questioning the depth to which I loved myself. I mean, I could say I loved myself, and I believed I loved myself. But the truth was, I was still unconsciously holding onto unsupportive stories (and patterns)—remains of my past which were keeping me stuck, unable to open fully to the love I desired and knew was available to me.

Loving ourselves is more than positive self-talk, mirror work, and mantras. Loving ourselves means accepting and honoring all of our parts, including the pieces we're ashamed to admit exist or let others see. It means befriending our inner critic, and knowing when to silence our ego to make room for our truth to come forward. It's about choosing ourselves in every moment, especially when it's an unpopular choice and goes against the grain, so to speak. Loving ourselves is a moment-by-moment practice that, at times, may feel challenging to accomplish. But you're worth it. We all are!

I used to feel embarrassed by the depth of which I loved, but I now realize that my ability to love even the darkest parts of another human soul is what makes me uniquely me, and it's become one of my favorite parts about myself. Loving others deeply had always come easily to me, but loving myself deeply after my assault took conscious and confronting work. If this is you, too, you're not alone.

You know that guy I mentioned dating who cheated on me over and over again? He was a huge mirror for me, reflecting back the rock-bottom place I'd sunk to (which I thankfully eventually found my way out of). But I stood in that shitty hole of a relationship for years, making excuses for his behavior, forgiving him and turning my back to his lies (although I definitely knew better). I even went to the hospital on the day his daughter was born to support him while he sat in the room with the woman he'd cheated on me with whom he'd gotten pregnant *while we were together.* Yeah, follow that track backward. That's some fucked up shit. But that's what I believed I deserved at the time because I was "the damaged one." I was "the broken one." I was "the dirty one." I had created an identity based on my experience, which was totally out of my control, labeling myself as *less than.* So *less than* is exactly what I got.

You see how that works? That's just one example of what can happen when we turn a blind eye to our needs and *choose out of* our personal relationship with ourselves in order to appease the egos of others. It's destructive, and oftentimes we don't even see what's happening until we've dug ourselves a hole so deep we can't see a way out.

But guess what? There's always a way out. And as much as it sucks to hear, the only way out is *through.* Meaning, you've gotta let yourself *feel the feelings* and do whatever's necessary to move the energy so that you can liberate yourself from your past and step into the present moment refreshed, ready to reconnect and re-engage with the life in front of you—fully connected with the person staring back at you in the mirror waiting to be loved *by you.*

Will I Ever Feel Safe to Let Love In?

Feeling safe begins with us, and our ability and willingness to know ourselves on a deep level. Letting love in becomes much easier once we've embraced our whole Self and have committed to the journey home to our truth.

It took me years to feel safe when receiving love. I longed for it, I sought it out, I chose partners I thought *could* love me, hoping that would be enough and that, eventually, I would learn to love me, too. But in the end, I realized the love I desired was never about another person. It was about reconnecting to my inner world, which meant I still had a lot of work to do. Once I allowed myself permission to forgive myself for staying silent for so long and accepting "mediocre love" to fill the spaces where pain lived, I was able to begin trusting myself and my decisions, which created the safety I yearned for. Thus, making room for more of what I desired to show up.

You are not your story–but *your story is absolutely part of you.* The sooner you decide you are no longer willing to accept whatever comes your way just to take up space in your life, the sooner you will begin to feel safe within yourself, your true home, where love has always been and will always be.

So start there. Start with your relationship between *you* and *you*. Commit to loving yourself deep in your bones, refusing to settle for crumbs—instead, demanding to experience all that life has to offer. It's available when you're ready and willing to say *yes to loving you.*

10

What Was It For?

"The best day of your life if the one on which you decide your life is your own. No apologies or excuses. No one to rely on or blame. The gift is yours, it's an amazing journey and you alone are responsible for the quality of it."
– Bob Moawad

My Nana was the most influential person in my life (aside from my brave and resilient mama). Losing her in 2019 was a punch to my gut and left a gaping hole I knew could never be filled. She was just a month shy of her 91st birthday when she left this physical plane, and on the morning I received the phone call that she was gone, I already knew in my heart she had taken her last breath. We were connected beyond what I can express in words, and the reality that I would never get to speak with her again, feel her big bear hugs, or hear her contagious laugh, nearly broke me.

She was everything to me. Writing this now, I can feel her with me, as the tears catch in the corners of my eyes and a smile finds my lips. She was the most amazing woman, and I am fortunate we chose each other (again) in this lifetime. She (Willa Mae) is the reason I am who I am in so many ways, which is why I am giving her story the well-deserved space to breathe through the pages to follow. Because without her, I'm not sure I could have managed being raped (and forgiving my rapist) with such grace.

Writing this book was made possible because of the belief my mom and my Nana both had in me. I realize not everyone has that. So if you don't, and finding support in your circle is hard or seemingly impossible, here's an invitation to borrow my belief in you for as long as you need it.

I know this journey can bring up a ton of emotions. I know how it feels to be on top of the world one day, only to be in the depths of despair the next. But I also know what it feels like to be free of the cycle of silence, which means it's available to you, too. So even if it feels like a pipe dream to heal and start over, as a whole person, please believe my words when I say: it's not...you can...and if you stay the course, you will be so proud you didn't give up.

The Road Less Traveled

Willa Mae was not a typical 1920s woman. She was fiercely independent, outspoken, opinionated, and deeply introspective. Her brother died when he was just four years old from appendicitis, leaving her parents with three very different little girls to raise, along with a void my grandmother worked hard to fill. Despite being beautiful and elegant in every sense of the word, she was a tomboy at heart, and took pride in her tree climbing abilities. She was affectionately known as "Billie" to her family and close friends, going above and beyond to make her dad proud as the fill-in son he'd so desperately wanted and had lost.

Despite being a tomboy growing up, she became a model in her twenties. And although marriage was the last thing on her mind (with many turned-down proposals, I might add), everything changed when Leo Stewart Trask walked into the picture. Or, shall I say, almost ran her over in the crosswalk! One of my favorite stories, really.

My grandmother was on a break from work one afternoon, and as she walked across the street back to her office, a handsome man drove by and nearly knocked her down. This wasn't uncommon as she was quite the looker! The driver of that car paid close attention to where she'd gone and soon after returning to her office, Leo walked in the door apologizing profusely and asked if he could take her to coffee. "Only if you take the whole office," she replied.

That was my Nana. Direct. Confident. Always wanting to include everyone. Not only was she beautiful inside and out, she was known for keeping people on their toes! It was on that day in 1954 when the love affair began between my vivacious grandmother and my suave grandfather. Just three short months later, they were married in a small ceremony and became pregnant immediately after.

Her marriage to my grandfather, while exciting in many ways, was not easy. Together they had three children (my mom being the baby and only girl), and although my grandmother yearned to explore the world and all it had to offer, she took on the role of mother, wife, and homemaker—the matriarch of the family—leaving many of her adventurous dreams behind. She loved the life she'd chosen, but she often spoke about the things she'd wished she'd been able to do... something she projected onto me growing up, encouraging me to say yes to life, yes to myself, and yes to the world around me at every chance.

My grandfather was a great man, but like all of us, he had his demons. He went through periods of drinking far too much, usually during the holidays, which left my classy and conservative grandmother heartbroken and ashamed, leaving her to pick up the pieces. He had a sharp tongue when he drank, and anyone who got in his way during these binges felt his wrath. But he loved our family and my grandmother wholly and completely. While much of their marriage was unconventional, they held onto their programming that said, "Til death do us part." And that's exactly what they did.

She was a free spirit, while he was a stereotypical blue-collar man. Together, they built a beautiful, modest home on two-and-a-half acres in the small town of Woodway, WA, being one of the first couples to settle into the area; now Woodway is full of expansive, multi-million-dollar homes. My grandmother made their property her sanctuary, which was such a special place to visit growing up. She was a talented landscaper, proudly featured in Sunset Magazine for her garden, a rambunctious collection of wild and carefree flowers, much like her. Nana loved hosting luncheons, entertaining, and showing her guests around her beloved "secret garden."

My grandfather, on the other hand, was more of an introvert, preferring to sit in front of the TV watching sports. He was a man of few words, but his heart was made of pure gold. He was so excited when I moved to San Diego, as he had fond memories of visiting the area when he was a gunner in the military, stories he'd often share during my visits back home.

While my grandmother and I were thick as thieves, it took a lot more effort to get to know my grandfather. Growing up, football Sundays were our time together, and although I didn't necessarily follow the game, I loved that this was our special time. Plus, it meant indulging in cinnamon rolls, or "sticky buns" as he called them, my favorite treat (even to this day).

Watching the ebbs and flows of their love showed me a lot about relationships, both the good and less than ideal. Although my grandfather was not a saint by any means, my grandmother never spoke ill of him and she always stood by him, something I admired deeply. She would try to shelter us grandkids from his alcohol-induced outbursts, but because I was the oldest (and the only girl), she shared more with me about the dynamics of their relationship, often cautioning me to "never rely on any man to support you," followed by, "travel as much and as often as you can…don't settle down with anyone until you are absolutely sure of their character," and so forth. I knew there was an ache in her heart that things had turned out the way they did when it came to his addiction, but there was also so much love, which I believe was challenging for her to accept at times.

She never thought the life she *had* was the life she'd *have*, yet here it was. And while I know she passed away with some regrets, she imparted the wisdom to leave it all on the table. To never settle. To live freely and unapologetically out loud!

She was incredibly intelligent, wildly curious, and carried a wisdom beyond anyone I've ever known. She continued to take classes until right before her death, always reminding me: "The moment we stop learning is the moment we die." She had the most courageous and beautiful spirit, and I miss her every single day.

My grandfather passed in his sleep lying beside my grandmother, hands intertwined, in 2011. And while I know this was hard for her (they were married for more than 56 years), I could sense a sort of peace about her after his death, as though she knew he was at peace and free to move into his next adventure, and she was ready to go on to hers, to fully experience what was left of her life.

Their marriage was far from perfect, but it was theirs. And it was beautiful. She taught me to find the lessons in everything, including the hard things. Relationships included.

When Life Hands You Lemons

"You make a damn good glass of lemonade!"

At least that's what my Nana always said. And you know what? She was right. Sometimes it may taste a little more sour than you'd like, but there's always an option to sweeten it (or as we often joked, add vodka if you're feeling frisky). And that's life, right?

We learn to adapt, and bend so we don't break. Inevitably, at some point we face the unexpected, and that's when having the tools necessary to consciously choose out of our circumstances and into something better are priceless.

Not quite two-and-a-half years after my grandfather passed, my feisty and tenacious grandmother's life would take a turn once again. This time, *choosing out* seemed an impossibility.

I'll never forget the phone call. I was walking into a Real Estate conference (my previous career while writing for a health and fitness magazine on the side) in Las Vegas, NV. My mom spoke in a worried rush on the other end.

"Sheree, Nana just had a stroke. We're at the hospital waiting to hear more from the doctors."

I felt like the air had been sucked from my lungs. I couldn't breathe or hear anything, despite being surrounded by loud slot machines, blaring music and rowdy party-goers. My world as I knew it closed in around me. This was the woman who ate "weeds" (as I called them as a child) from her garden, had done Tai Chi and yoga for decades, meditated daily, loved the shit outta life and her family, and beat cancer using mindset, movement and nutrition, stating: "Healing can always be found within us and within nature if we take the time to listen and honor what's really going on…" (her words, not mine). A stroke? How was that possible?

My inclination was to jump on the first plane to Seattle to be with my family, but my mom assured me it was best to stay in Las Vegas and finish my trip. She'd keep me posted on any progress as soon as she knew more.

I was devastated. The woman I thought of as indestructible was facing something massive, and it seemed completely out of our control. *What if she didn't make it? Did she know how much she meant to me? Did I say "I love you" enough?*

As thoughts swirled through my mind, I remembered the words she'd say to me every time I complained as a child or any time I'd been worried about anything as I got older: "Find the *for*." She always believed there was surely a purpose behind everything that happened in our lives. All I knew was that if anyone could get through this, it was her. I believed that. And she wouldn't have to go through any of it alone.

Re-Learning Old Things

Thankfully, she did come out of it alive, although partially paralyzed and unable to speak very well. For a woman with a helluva lot to say, this really pissed her off. I flew home to help care for her, sharing shifts with my mom each day for the next month. It was the most painful thing I've ever witnessed, to watch a capable and young-at-heart woman become dependent on others for her livelihood. And she despised it. Over and over again she begged to die, but I knew this was her pride talking, not her heart. She had way too much spirit left to leave on anyone else's terms but her own.

Days turned into weeks which turned into months, and eventually, through therapy and a lot of patience and practice, she found old words that had been tucked away deep in her mind, as well as small movements to help her feel a semblance of independence (although minor).

I missed our talks. I missed her laugh. I missed her hugs, which were so strong I often joked that she'd been lifting too much weight in the gym. I missed her joyful and infectious spirit, which I knew still existed somewhere in the forgotten pieces she was working so hard to remember.

We made the decision to move her from the home she and my grandfather had built from scratch as newlyweds, raising their babies and later sharing it with us grandkids, and into an independent living facility where she had the option of additional care as needed. She was surrounded by a group of amazing new friends and soon earned the title, "the life of the party," always bringing her curiosity, kindness, warm smile (and fortune cookies for all) with her, taking part in as many activities as possible, especially enjoying time in the pool, something she loved so much.

The next few years were tough, facing challenge after challenge on her path to healing. And at some point we were advised that this was as good as it was going to get—and it was time to accept the reality that she'd never walk again (liars), and she'd never speak either (you don't know my Nana). Well, she would be damned if she'd let their prognosis dictate her reality. She was fueled by her determination (and stubbornness), which, as it so happened, was exactly what was needed.

She fought long and hard. There were good days and then not-so-good ones. I found our roles reversing as I became the one to give her the tough love she'd always showered me with, using her words to negotiate behavior adjustments to bring her back to reality and out of her melancholy. I earned the nickname "drill sergeant," which she always followed with an eye roll and a giggle. She'd come so far, and we were all so proud of her. While this new status wasn't where she wanted to be, she was doing things the doctors swore were impossible given her age and the severity of the stroke. She was a true warrior.

Eventually, with the incredible support of her therapists and my absolutely amazing mom, she was able to walk with a walker, although slowly. And she was able to use her brilliant mind differently, learning to listen more closely and connect with people in ways that fully able-bodied people often don't do all that well. She was present, attuned, compassionate, and adored. Everyone who met her instantly loved her, and I felt so lucky that she was mine.

She could often be found on the 10th floor of her building, which she referred to as the Taj Mahal, pruning plants or telling people the "right" way to do so. She was a tough-love kind of teacher, but she was usually right. She carried her gardening shears with her everywhere she went. On walks around the property, she liked to "borrow" flowers from other peoples gardens claiming, "Oh, they won't mind!"

While most people thought of her as an angel on Earth (and she was), she had a quiet rebellious side, too (my favorite side). But always, her heart was in the right place.

Communication Beyond Words

After spending a few years in her new home at Bayview in Seattle, she enrolled in a class led by a young man around my age named Kevin Graybill. In this class, he took a group of 10 to 12 residents through his eight-week program: "Full Circle Dialogue Introductory Series." They met weekly for eight weeks while Kevin taught them various dialogue concepts/tools, which they would all practice together. She loved his class and had come to love him equally.

After she passed, I learned more about Kevin and the bond they'd formed during their time together. My mom shared with me how my Nana had encouraged him to pursue his dream of becoming a professional musician, which led him to going all in and *succeeding!* Her mantra was always "follow your bliss" (Joseph Campbell), and she encouraged everyone to do so, even people she barely knew.

In 2019, I reached out to Kevin on Facebook, wanting to know more about the man who my sweet Nana had spoken so highly about. Then in 2020, Kevin emailed me asking if he could share an article with me that he'd written about my grandmother, along with a voice recording he had of one of their sessions together. To this day, that recording is one of my most favorite and precious things.

The below was taken with permission from Kevin's blog post titled, *Communication Beyond Words,* which he wrote about my grandmother after her passing:

"On the first day while meeting all of the residents, aside from the common hearing and sight impairments of old age that most of them shared, I took note that one of the residents had suffered a stroke recently and struggled significantly with speaking. Initially, I was slightly anxious, thinking to myself, *"How is she going to participate? Is she going to enjoy this? How will I know if she's enjoying this?"* Having said that, as one week turned into the next, and I got to know each resident, especially this particular one, I came to find that she struggled with *speaking*, but she did not struggle one bit with *expressing herself.* It was very inspiring, and served as such a powerful reminder to me that there is so much more to communicating than words... About 5% of her communication was words, and the remaining 95% was tone, inflection, and body language and amazingly, I always understood her!

We need words to *explain* complex concepts, but *expressing* feelings is a whole different story, and she was always able to successfully express to me how she was feeling throughout the entire process. Tone, inflection, and body language are all very effective ways to express how one feels, and when combined, they can be exponentially more powerful than words.

After one of our weekly sessions, she combined all three by approaching me, gently grabbing my hands, smiling, looking me in the eyes, and she then spent a minute or two struggling to get out the words, "*I appreciate you being here*" with such a transparently kind tone and inflection. When people can just use words, they tend to not be as intentional with their tone, inflection, and body language, because they don't feel that they *need* to. Words can be the ultimate shortcut in a way, but the lengths that this resident was forced to go to to express herself to me, proved to have been a much more powerful way to communicate than if she just casually said "*I appreciate you being here*" on her way out the door.

It was interesting to me that at the beginning of the eight week series, I looked at her as if she was impaired because she wasn't able to *explain* things very well sometimes. Due to her "*explanatory difficulties*" though, she had become exceptionally gifted at *expressing* herself through other means still available to her."

While it's true that what we say matters, equally—if not, more important—is how we say it. My sweet Nana was proof that verbalizing ourselves audibly was not the only way to create powerful connections.

The thing is, no matter where we are in our lives, we are faced with a series of choice-points. We can either give in to the stories, or we can rise above our circumstances. But we can't do both, at least not simultaneously.

My grandmother lived her life unapologetically, fully embodied in her truest expression of love and kindness. She did not let her past define her present, although at times, a struggle between the two definitely ensued. She was a force to be reckoned with, and it was obvious to not only those who knew her but also to strangers who could feel the power in her presence.

The last year of her life, we talked a lot about death in our visits together, but also about her dreams for me and my future. I know she was proud of me, and that's all I could ever hope for. She would've given anything to see me walk down the aisle, which I often teased her about given her conviction that I remain "strong and independent" and reminded me constantly not to "rely on a man for anything." Now that the end was near (or simply a new beginning, however you choose to see it), she just wanted to know that I would be taken care of. I also believe she wanted to be sure I would be loved by a partner deeply, just as she loved me.

The last visit I had with her, before things really took a turn, I was able to read her the eulogy I'd written for her. We cried together as I poured my heart out, and in this precious moment I knew that would be the last time we'd be together in this way. I think she knew it, too.

Choose Out of Suffering

So much of what my grandmother experienced could have taken her down a much different path. Instead, she *chose out* of suffering and *into peace.* I wish I'd asked her more about the foundation for her way of thinking and being in the world. I mean, she was born in 1928, not exactly the time of the outspoken, independent woman! I do know, however, that she adored Joseph Campbell who wrote in detail about the human experience, which she read to me as bedtime stories growing up. My Nana was diligent about being conscious of her mindset, and turned to understanding other cultures as a way to form opinions and find the path that suited her beliefs best, based on the outcomes she desired—all of which was made apparent in the way she showed up and loved the world.

In Gabby Bernstein's book *Super Attractor*, she talks about the *Abraham-Hicks Emotional Guidance Scale.* Although my grandmother didn't know who Gabby Bernstein was, and likely was unaware of the Abraham-Hicks teachings, this scale emulates exactly how she lived her life.

Without going into all the details, the Emotional Guidance Scale is a scale of our feelings and emotions, going from our highest feeling states (such as joy) to our lowest feeling states (such as powerlessness). The idea suggests when we feel emotions that register lower on the scale, in order to reach for the next rung on the ladder, if you will, we must gradually reach upward to move into a better feeling state.

Now, if you're at your lowest point, reaching for the highest emotion on the scale will seem unattainable and misaligned to your truth. So, instead of jumping to the top, this is an invitation to reach for the state just one emotion above your current feeling. Repeating this process until we've reached our desired feeling allows us to climb out of our negative emotions, bringing us closer to our highest feeling state in a safe and authentic way. This may happen quickly or, for some, more slowly. Neither is right or wrong. The point is not to chase the better feeling and skip the journey to get there, instead experiencing the emotional stages wholly while choosing better feelings continuously in whatever way feels true for you.

I've mentioned before that "like attracts like." Using this scale to manage your level of magnetism to things, people and experiences in your current reality can be eye-opening and a great motivator to choose differently (better) in any given moment. If this is new for you, it might feel challenging at first. Honestly, even if you're a seasoned "climber," there may be times where it feels downright hard. Just remember, as with anything, this moment is temporary. And always, there is a way out.

When Joy Feels Wrong

It's true that sometimes we may desire to feel a more uplifting emotion, while holding onto a lower vibrational feeling. While this may feel confusing and counterproductive to our desired outcome, during these times I have trained myself to ask, "What am I so afraid of?" Usually, what comes up has nothing to do with releasing the emotion itself, but with my fear of letting go and having to step into the unknown.

Change is scary, emotions (and the unknown) included. But when we remember that we are here to experience the full spectrum of what it means to be human, we can choose to find gratitude in each moment, or we can choose to harden to life. In my experience, choosing the highest feeling we're capable of is often what's needed to keep going, instead of getting stuck in the doom and gloom, which never feels good.

Of course, there are times when this seems impossible. There are also times where we may feel a sense of guilt for feeling better, especially when something terrible has happened (such as the death of a loved one) or we're being asked to release an emotion that we have attached our identity to (i.e., *I am a rape "victim" so I should feel angry, dirty and broken, not happy, at peace and joyful*).

Choosing out of something you don't want (such as pain), is ultimately choosing *into* something you do want (such as joy). When we are conscious of these choices, and aware of our patterns in these moments, we can continue to shift as needed to align deeper with our truth, becoming a magnet to attract what's truly meant for us. Receiving, then, becomes the real invitation and begs the question, *Can you (will you) allow yourself to experience all that's available to you? Or will you close yourself in an effort to remain the same?*

What Was It For?

"Find the for."

I have lived by this statement from my Nana my entire life, seeking reasoning, at times, to things that seemingly have no answer. But sometimes the lesson is the experience itself, and trying to dig deeper and deeper to uncover *more* doesn't actually serve our hearts at all.

Sometimes, shitty things happen to really good people. It sucks. It's not fair. And I wish it weren't the case. But if I've learned anything along my journey home, back to myself, it's this:

We are often stronger than we think and more capable than we give ourselves credit for.

And that includes you reading this book right now.

At this point, I hope you can see that trauma covers a wide spectrum of emotions and experiences—expressed, withheld, and dealt with on an incredibly personal level. We shame ourselves for not *getting over it fast enough*, failing to celebrate ourselves for surviving the madness in the first place. I see this as a missed opportunity for healing and expansion.

Healing is not a linear path, it's a process. And if we allow it, the process can be quite rewarding. No matter the stage you're in, the questions will continue to come, and sometimes the answers will follow. Other times, we learn to trust our resilience and our ability to overcome even the things we did not choose and cannot change. We don't have to like what happened, but if we truly want to be free, there is a level of acceptance we must embrace to move on and begin living again. The version of ourselves that emerges after trauma (sexual or otherwise) is often foreign and, at times, perplexing to befriend.

Although we cannot control all things, we can control the most important thing, and according to my Nana this is... *our mind.* As you take this next step into the life you're creating, I invite you to be an active participant in the process. Even the uncomfortable parts. There is magic there.

Instead of beating yourself up for not knowing the answers, choose *out* of the blame, shame and guilt cycle and *into* love and acceptance. You will get through this. You are capable. You are worthy. And you're never alone.

What was it for? I'm not sure...you tell me. Inevitably, you're in charge of your thinking. And nobody can take that away from you.

Hold the standard high for yourself and your life. Because the only thing holding you back is you...

Until now.

"What you get in your life is what you have in your heart.
I have the loveliest life in the world."
– Willa Mae Trask

Closure

"Not everything that is faced can be changed, but nothing can be changed until it's faced." – James Baldwin

In Chapter 2, I asked you a big question regarding your continued hurt and pain: *Why are you choosing to keep it?* Not a moment of judgment, but an honest question that I would encourage you to sit with for a time, no matter how scary or uncomfortable it may seem. You see, it wasn't until I was able to consciously admit to myself that I was *choosing* to keep my pain out of fear that I had *no idea who I was without it*, that I was able to dive in and do the work to release the lingering pieces of my past hurt, and begin to truly live again. I want this for you, too.

Since coming to terms with where I was holding myself back, and deciding that I was no longer willing to put a cap on my present day happiness simply because I had previously been hurt, my world as I knew it opened in ways I never thought possible. When I stopped basing my existence on the trauma I'd endured, instead focusing on the woman I had become in the process of moving through all the bullshit, I found peace. And with that peace came a whisper from within that said...

You can move on now, warrior. You can be strong and soft at the same time. You are safe to take up space. You can still help people without being tied to your story. You are who you are because of what you've been through and the woman I know is brave, bold, and brilliant. You are free to soar, sweet girl. Your mom and Nana are so proud of you. I'm proud of you, too.

While in many ways my story has shifted and evolved as I have, my purpose has not wavered. I am more committed now than ever before to helping people step into their truth and use their voices and stories to heal. I am fiercely determined to do my part to help us all come together to not only heal ourselves, but to heal the collective as well so we can all experience an abundance of joy and freedom. My story no longer dictates how I move through the world—it is not something I wear as a cloak of protection against possible future pain, while I run myself into the ground trying to "prove" my worth.

I am worthy because I exist—and so are you.

Trauma or not, we all have a story. And our stories are powerful. I firmly believe our stories are necessary—whether we share them openly or not—as they connect us to one another, and show us that we're not alone. While I cannot physically be there to hold your hand as you courageously move through your own healing journey, I hope this book has served as a friend of sorts, holding you through your pain as you step into more peace.

Although I have chosen to start living my life free from the weight of my story, rewriting my painful experiences so as not to base my entire existence on my past, in no way does that mean I've forgotten where I came from (and healed from) or what I'm here to do. I am inviting you to take a similar approach—one that resonates with you and feels empowering as you open yourself up to possibility. Because the truth is, there's still time. It's not too late. And you deserve to feel whole.

Release

Finalizing my memoir has been bittersweet, and a long time coming. I started and stopped more times than I'd like to admit over the years, as I continued to lean in and listen to my soul that kept whispering, *not yet,* despite my desire to complete this journey. But with the chaos and uncertainty made possible by 2020 (and a worldwide pandemic), something shifted, and I could feel the end transforming into a new beginning—my next "chapter," ready to emerge.

As I write this chapter now, looking through the wide floor-to-ceiling windows of my office, peering out at the bright green trees swaying in the wind and the big blue sky above, there are birds chirping while classical music plays softly in the background. My home is surrounded by boxes, signaling yet another chapter closing in conjunction with the completion of this book, as I prepare to move in with the man of my dreams, a love I'd always hoped for and waited nearly 40 years to find.

With the closing of both of these chapters—this book and my physical home—as I mentioned, I also made the decision to stop using my story of rape as the catalyst to connect to others, on social platforms and beyond. For decades it's been part of my "signature story," and while it will always be an enormous part of my *becoming*, it no longer feels aligned to highlight. Rape is not who I am, it's something that happened…and it doesn't define me. I will continue to remain an advocate for vulnerable conversations and to stand beside my fellow survivors, but I no longer feel called to hold onto my rape story as part of my identity and the thing that connects me to my fellow warriors. I can now willingly share my story…without feeling the need to do so.

The decision to release my story *for good* stemmed from a session with an energy healer. I mentioned to her the energetic depletion I felt around regurgitating this story over and over again, and I shared with her the responsibility I felt in doing so because I knew it had served to support so many others over the years. I realized that my story had become one of the defining through-lines of my work for so long, and I didn't want to hold it anymore. It felt heavy and no longer empowering. That session ended with my healer giving me the permission I didn't know I needed to let it go. So I am doing the same for you right now.

If it's heavy, *put it down.* You've held it long enough. This is your permission to be free, warrior.

I carried pride with my story for years, and I am glad that my vulnerability supported so many on their own healing paths. But I feel complete now. This doesn't mean I will never speak about it again, or that I no longer stand alongside the other brave souls showing up so courageously in their pain and power. What it means for me is the acknowledgement that I have used my story to do great things, including creating positive change for other survivors and the way they see and share their stories. But I don't have to identify as a "survivor" anymore. This label used to empower me—but after two decades, it's become exhausting.

So I'm done—I feel a sense of completion and closure. Possibly like you, I am someone who's overcome a great deal in my life. And largely because of my experiences with trauma, I have the tremendous honor of supporting others through my work by bravely sharing their stories of resilience and hope. But I have chosen to release the responsibility I was carrying which said that I had to constantly relive my trauma in order to fulfill my purpose. I now know I can live freely as a healed woman without attaching a label—such as *rape survivor*—to my story. And at the same time, I can continue to help others heal by showing them what's available on the other side of all the pain.

Trauma fatigue is real and wow, did I have a case of the sleepies! I am finally ready to step into the next chapter of my life, energized and fully open to whatever's next. I can still hold space for courageous stories to unfold—but with this book...I've told mine, and I recognize that I no longer need to keep playing that old record on repeat.

If this resonates with you, I've left a couple offerings at the end of this chapter that may support you in letting go so you can move on, too, once and for all. This doesn't mean we forget, as I don't think that's possible to do. Define "letting go" however you'd like, but choose your definition and subsequent actions from a place of power versus obligation or expectation. You've been through enough. Now it's your time to fly and create the life of your choosing.

Home Is Within

It was January 1, 2020. I holed myself up in an adorable Airbnb in San Clemente, CA after putting all of my belongings in a storage unit months prior when I realized I had become too attached to *home* as a place versus what home really is…a soul-relationship between me and me. I'd been a nomad for a while, with my homebase being one of my best friend's spare rooms while I bounced around from place to place getting to know myself without a physical home. As I awoke to the sunlight piercing through the white linen curtains of the very zen bedroom on the first day of a brand new year, something within told me this cycle was coming to a close, and I felt a sense of calm permeate my entire being. I was ready to feel settled in my environment, just as I now did in my body and mind.

It was my last day in this sweet little beach town, so I went for a morning walk, grabbed a bite to eat while enjoying the crisp Southern California "winter" (you know…68 degrees and sunny), and got my vanilla latté with oat milk to go so I could head back to the little studio I'd rented and do what I had done for years every January 1st.

While I don't do resolutions, I am a big believer in intentions and creating the life we desire. And since I'm a writer by trade, writing is my modality of choice when setting out to create anything deeply meaningful.

As soon as I walked in the door of my temporary "home," I put on some music, sat on the bed, closed my eyes and asked myself: *What do you want this year to look like? Feel like? Taste like? Smell like? Who do you want to share these experiences with?*

After a few moments in silence, I grabbed my laptop and began to write. If you've ever seen the GIF of Kermit the Frog furiously typing away on his keyboard, that was me. (And if you haven't, Google it for a laugh.)

I wrote everything down in present tense *as if it already existed.* I talked about falling in love, continuing to support incredible change-makers with writing their books, creating an impact through stories (mine and other peoples), spending time with loved ones, traveling, and described in detail the "home" I was ready to call into my reality.

Acting "as if" is one of my favorite hacks, because it tricks the brain in the best way. It also helps align the frequency of thought and action, making it more likely for these desires to come to fruition.

Within 24 hours, I was on Zillow and wouldn't you know, there it was...my new home! From the moment I opened the listing, I knew this was it, and I reached out to the agent immediately. Two weeks later, I moved into my cozy little treehouse, filled with natural light, merely blocks to the beach. Just in time, too, because it was only a couple months later that the whole world shut down, paralyzed by fear of the unknown during the pandemic.

For me, my treehouse has been so much more than somewhere to eat and sleep. It's truly been a place of healing and transformation for me. I had my best year in business in this home. I met the love of my life while living in this home. I got to become an auntie to 12 pandemic babies in this home. (I just noticed there's a theme of "12" throughout this book, I wonder what that means?) And yes, I said *12 babies.* Apparently, the pandemic was an aphrodisiac for some. Or people got bored. Whatever the case, magic happened while living in this home, and I will be forever grateful.

To the home that has held me through transformation and becoming, thank you. What a gift you've been.

Opening to Love

Anyone who was single when the pandemic hit surely had at least a brief moment of panic (if they were someone desiring partnership, that is). *How am I supposed to meet people now?*

I don't know about everywhere else in the world, but here in San Diego, things definitely shut down for a while, which wasn't really conducive to the letter I'd written at the start of the year. In that letter, I'd said this was the year I would meet the man of my dreams, fall in love, and live happily ever after. There was no time for a pandemic!

I won't share our love story here because this book isn't about that, and some things…well, I prefer to keep them private. But I will say that meeting him was the icing on the cake to a long journey back home to myself. And I truly believe that it was only possible because of my commitment to do the work, no matter how hard it may have been.

I'd spent countless hours implementing all the things I'd learned over the years, and I felt ready to open fully to another person. I desired partnership, and finally the thought of carrying it didn't feel heavy anymore, or like something I was chasing to complete me. Instead, it felt like freedom and another choice point to *choose into* something amazing!

Standing outside of the sushi restaurant in Del Mar, CA a couple of weeks after our initial online encounter via Bumble, I watched this man walk towards me, masked (due to pandemic regulations), and I knew in an instant that he was different. Yet even after an amazing first date, I questioned whether or not to go out with him again, which is funny to me now. He embodied everything I had ever dreamed of and so much more, but there was still an old record playing inside that questioned, *Can I really have this?*

I am so glad that I let myself explore possibility with him, and I pinch myself thinking about how truly blessed I am to have such an incredible man in my life. He holds my stories with care, void of judgment, and pours love into me daily. I am beyond lucky, and not a day goes by that I don't thank God for this man. I also give myself a high five from time to time for releasing my past pain so I could be free to love and be loved in this way. Because damn, it was a lot of work!

I may have been 39 years old when we met, but it was all in perfect timing. The years I spent wondering if love would ever be mine all made sense now. All the heartache I'd experienced–all the pain, illness, setbacks, and silence–every single thing in my life made sense as if he was the missing puzzle piece I never knew I needed. He felt like home from the moment our eyes connected. He was the man I'd always believed existed, but had yet to meet until that warm and breezy evening in September. And I love him to the depths of my existence and beyond. I wrote this a few months after we began dating, and it still gives me butterflies to read because it's true, now more than ever.

He's loving me whole
But not in the sense that I was ever broken
Because I've always been here
Although scattered in pieces
All of me, within
The glue that I needed
Was simply his love
Giving me strength and courage
To fight the inner battles
Keeping me separate from myself
While I was grasping in desperation
Just to be whole

Thank you for finding me, my love. I love you the most.

Final Pep Talk

All that you desire is available, dear reader. When things feel impossible or seem too hard, come back home to yourself and focus on what's real—*you are enough as you are.* What you seek is within, so take the time to get to know her, honor her, and love her fully. Everything will fall into place as you continue to show up, authentically, and love the world deeply through simply being you.

Because you, sweet soul, are pure magic. You are brave, courageous, inspiring, worthy, whole, complete, and so incredibly beautiful, inside and out. Your seemingly broken pieces make it possible for the light to shine outward and lead others home. And more importantly, these are the very things that will help you guide yourself home, too. The responsibility that we so often carry as survivors to show up in the world "put together" can feel staggering and overwhelming. But I am here to remind you that your path to healing is yours, and there is no right or wrong way to go about it.

Throughout these pages I have shared with you my personal journey through the mess and into the magic. As you can see, I don't believe in avoiding our shit if we truly want to be free and live a purpose-filled life. I want you to be free, warrior. And I believe that somewhere within your beautiful soul, you want that freedom, too.

Somewhere along the way, maybe you told yourself it wasn't possible. Maybe staying in the pain has actually felt soothing because it's provided proof that what happened was real, and that proof helps you make sense of things. Maybe your attachment to your wounds, and the emotions your story brings, reminds you of your strength. Maybe without it, you feel weak. Maybe you believe that if people knew the truth, they would judge you or leave you...possibly both.

All of this, or none of this, may be true. But through it all, you survived...you are still here...and you are, always, worthy of everything your heart desires.

In Closing

It's okay if you find yourself in all the feels. It's okay if you decide, *Nope, not today, feelings!* And it's okay if you oscillate between being on top of the world and down in the dumps. What matters is that you let yourself be with what arises and *choose in* and *choose out* accordingly, using healthy coping tools (some of which I've shared in this book) to move you forward at whatever pace feels safe and true for you.

Sometimes it's the simplest things that allow for the greatest expansion, so don't close yourself to simplicity when it invites you in for tea. Find the thing(s) that support your nervous system and aid you in reaching equanimity. Homeostasis is possible, even if you're someone who has become addicted to the struggle, or finds herself feeling chaotic and imbalanced on the regular. Give yourself grace and love yourself up. This process is a journey. Be present for the ride. I promise, it doesn't have to be all shit. There's plenty of beauty available when you open your eyes and take a good look at how far you've come.

Here are a couple practices I learned from one of my energy healers to help you close the gap and release any stagnant energy that may be lingering so that you can heal, fully and completely.

Candle Closure Ceremony

This simple practice can be so powerful so even if it seems silly or strange, I'm inviting you to try something new, out of your comfort zone, and remain open. The worst that can happen is...nothing. So go for it! Say *yes* to possibility, warrior.

1. State your intention. *(What do you want to let go of? Heal?)*
2. Take two small-ish candles (tall/thin or birthday candles will work, too) and place them next to each other; one is *you*, the other is the *story* you can't seem to let go of.

3. Then tie a thin string around the candles to connect them at the midway point and light the candles, allowing them to burn and sever their tie to each other.
4. State your intention again, although now in present-tense. *(i.e. I am free of my story)*
5. Now go be free, warrior. And live the life waiting for you.

Write a Closure Letter

This can be to a person, experience, whatever you're holding onto that you want to release. Be intentional. Just as with the candle ceremony above, the idea is for you to be honest and vulnerable with yourself and allow yourself to let go. It doesn't have to be long, or complicated. Let it be whatever it is.

Here's the one I wrote:

Dear rape,

I now release the vow I made, to use my pain for a purpose for all of my days. I did what I said I would do (create positive change), and now I am ready to close this chapter and move on to my next mission. I am proud of the way I showed up to help myself and others heal.

Thank you.
I am now complete.

I love you,
Sheree

Be Free, Warrior

It's been my honor and privilege to be with you on this leg of your journey, wherever you happen to be. Through these pages, I've opened myself to you in hopes that you will begin to comprehend just how *seen* you are—even if the support feels intangible. Holding your story so tightly can feel heavy and burdensome—I know because I did it for years. So again, I invite you to open your heart to possibility, and grant yourself permission to release…let go…put it down—and make room for a new, better feeling story to unfold.

We are the brave ones who, despite our odds, managed to keep our shit together and persevere. We may have been messy as we unraveled pieces of ourselves in the process of trying to understand the reasoning behind it all. Yet, here we are—you and me. We made it! And while we're all imperfect in our own right, I've come to understand that it's within the imperfection that our perfect story *for us* is made possible. We don't have to like all of it, but the sooner we can accept it for what it is—*ours*—the better off we'll be as we move forward with courage and strength.

As you go forth into the next chapter of your story, I hope you'll come back to this book and remember just how loved and supported you are. I don't have to know you personally to love you wholly—I love you simply because you exist. It's time that you gave that same love to yourself for that simple, yet profound reason, too.

Surviving Silence: A Companion Journal

"Confront the dark parts of yourself, and work to banish them with illumination and forgiveness. Your willingness to wrestle with your demons will cause your angels to sing."
– August Wilson

Dear Reader,

I hope this book has served you beautifully, in whatever way it was meant to touch your life. I hope that you feel a deeper sense of optimism, and a newfound peace about your journey and the future that still awaits your courageous spirit.

I hope you can see that no matter where you've been, you can overcome even the most challenging circumstances because you're strong and resilient—far more than you've been led to believe. While it's true that you may not always understand why what happened, happened...I hope you can begin to accept that there's a purpose within, even if none of it makes any sense right now. Maybe you're not meant to understand why things occurred the way they did (or are still unfolding the way they are right now). Regardless, I am asking you to be brave and let the unknown settle into your bones—and find a way to be okay with the uncertainty.

I hope you can rest a little easier knowing that you're not alone, and although our individual journey's may be different, the questions we (survivors) ask ourselves in the process of healing are likely more similar than we'd like to admit.

I hope you will allow yourself to identify any lingering confusion as an invitation to trust the process and continue persevering, in spite of your traumas and hardships.

You are capable of healing—and you can get through anything...even this.

With so much chaos in the world, I hope this book has been a source of inspiration—showing you what's possible on the other side of the pain, and possibly what's on the other side of your secrets, too. I know some of the content may have been hard to read. It may have triggered old stories, or parts of you that have been tucked away for a long time. Thank you for witnessing my journey amidst your own vulnerable unfolding. I hope my story has provided you with beneficial, tangible tools to use as you bravely step into the life waiting for you at whatever pace feels right *for you.*

I hope this book has allowed you to feel seen and understood in new ways that will carry you forward as you continue opening yourself up to life—becoming more of *you* each and every day.

I hope you know how valuable you are, and that you can see how truly worthy of love, happiness, and wholeness you are now—and have always been. Let this be a new beginning...a place to set your worries down, releasing anything that feels too heavy to bear any longer. You are safe to let go. You are safe to heal. You are safe to be unapologetically *you.*

The Questions

Below are the primary questions I asked throughout the book, chapter by chapter. Use this companion journal as a guide to further assist you in your healing, as you learn to not only accept, but *love* your story, however it feels aligned and nourishing for you to do so.

Don't rush the answers to these questions. Instead, be intentional with your time as you sit with each question (for however long it takes) and allow your body to speak through your fingertips, writing as much or as little as you need to feel complete before moving onto the next question, and the next.

There are no "right" answers. Whatever answers feel true for you are perfect. As you heal more deeply, you may notice your answers changing—welcome whatever change wants to come with open arms, and an open heart. Your evolution is a sign of your willingness to let go and offer the weight of your pain to the Universe. Your courage is admirable and deserving of celebration.

Use this journal as a safe space to open yourself to love, and whatever wants to come through as you rest in the stillness of your truth. You may feel anger rise up...you may feel sadness or grief...even waves of joy and laughter. Let these emotions come, void of judgment. Instead, get curious. Ask your emotions, *What are you here to teach me? What do you want me to know in this moment?* Then close your eyes and be with yourself in the vast open space of the unknown. Allow the tide of emotions to wash over you and when you're ready, grant yourself permission to *let...them...go.*

This experience is yours, nobody else's. The thoughts and opinions of others are not welcome here. Let this be a sacred space for further healing to occur.

The time it will take to get on the other side of your pain is individual. If it takes longer than you'd like, let this be an invitation to practice patience and self-compassion—not frustration. Being attached to a specific timeframe to be "healed" often brings frustration so if that's the case for you, release this limitation now. Be available for whatever is working its way toward you, in an effort to fill you up, as you courageously leave behind what you no longer need.

We often feel tested when our timing doesn't coincide with our ego's schedule. This is a brilliant place to become an observer in your experience and again, get curious. Ask yourself, *Why do I feel frustrated by this? What would make me feel more at ease?* Thank the Universe (or what/whomever you resonate with) for these signals, and breathe into the space of the unknown as you continue to empty and be filled up by love.

Let your tears fall if they come, leaving behind more room for what you wish to feel, experience and receive. "Tears are what happen when the ice in the heart melts." — Tosha Silver

This journey is yours for the taking, my dear. It's time to reclaim your power and say yes to healing—and yes to your life.

I believe in you and I am so proud of you.
I know you can do this. You deserve to be free—and you don't have to do any of it alone.

To your healing with love,

Sheree

Journal Prompts

Chapter 1: Why Me?

1. Is how I feel right now supporting where I want to go?
2. If I were free of (*pain, anger, sadness, grief*), how would my life improve?
3. How do I want to feel instead?
4. How much longer am I willing to stay stuck here before I decide to move in the direction of my dreams, and choose a better feeling state?

Chapter 2: What Was Harming Them?

1. Is the stuckness you're choosing worth the expansion you're blocking?
2. If not, then what are you willing to release to feel the emotions you desire and create a new story?

3. What does forgiveness mean to you?
4. How do you stretch towards forgiveness instead of away from love?
5. What would it look like, feel like to be free of the pain you're still holding onto?
6. What is your freedom worth?

Chapter 3: Who Am I Now?

Write a letter to the version of you that existed before you were hurt.

1. What do you want the past *you* to know?
2. What are you holding onto that needs to be released?

Tell her. And remind her she's safe to emote, express, and experience all that life has in store from this moment forward.

This is your invitation to start over, and believe that the best is yet to come.

Because who you are is whoever you decide to be. So be free. Be wild. Be authentically and unapologetically YOU. And trust that it's enough… because you are enough… you always will be.

Chapter 4: Is It Possible To Love My Broken Parts?

I want you to ask yourself the following questions without shame, blame, guilt or judgment. This is not about being a victim, this is about creating awareness so you can create something better moving forward. Take 20 minutes or so and go through this exercise. You may be surprised as to what comes up.

Here are some prompts to move you into your truth so you can shift as needed…

1. **What stories are you still holding onto from your past that are keeping you stuck today?** *Examples could be: I'm not smart enough; I will never make a ton of money; Money is for assholes, and I'm not an asshole; Nobody wants to hear what I have to say; I'm not worthy of abundance or having an amazing life; I'm unlovable…everybody leaves me.*
2. **Where do these beliefs come from?** *This is a massive awareness point that often feels really scary to dive into and admit. Totally okay. Be with whatever comes up. It could be something or someone in your childhood; it could be from a past experience. Dig deep and find the dirt!*
3. **How are these beliefs holding me back?** *Examples: Because of this belief, I don't trust people… I keep my guard up… My body is breaking down… I'm broke and unhappy… I'm single…*

Now for the fun part—the reframe! This is where you get to reprogram your subconscious and tell it a new, more empowering story, one that feels supportive and most importantly true!

You'll probably slip up along the way because, you know, this whole *human* thing. Give yourself a break though. Those thoughts taking up space in your head won't just change overnight. I mean, think of all the years it's taken to nail down the beliefs you have right now!

The good news is it's up to *you* to rewrite that story. So get after it! You can, and you will, if you really want to. But that's your call.

Instead of (insert limiting belief).
I am choosing (insert new belief: the reframe).

Repeat this with as many limiting beliefs as you can think of, and see how you feel once you've let it all out and have inserted a new belief in its place.

Chapter 5: Can I Be Courageous Enough to Be Seen?

1. What is hiding costing you?
2. What do you imagine living out loud (fully expressed) would look like… feel like for you?

Chapter 6: Will I Ever Feel Like I'm Enough?

1. What makes you believe you're not enough?
2. Who told you that you needed to earn your keep (your worth was dependent on it)?
3. Are you willing to drop any outdated beliefs to make room for better feeling beliefs to take up space?
4. When you think about the life you want, what does it look, feel, smell, and taste like? (write these things down!)

Chapter 7: Can I Be Brave Enough to Speak My Truth?

1. How long am I willing to carry the weight of this pain?
2. What would feel better in its place?
3. Can I give myself the permission I've been seeking (possibly through external circumstances) and finally let it all go?

Here are some statements/questions to consider when you decide to open the dialogue with your loved ones about your experience (or theirs)...

I have something I'd like to share with you. It feels heavy so I want to make sure you have the capacity to be with me as I open myself to you. Is now a good time?

Something's been weighing on me and it feels really scary to share. I'm afraid you might see me differently, stop loving me, or leave me (fill this with whatever feels true for you). My words feel shaky right now but I really need to get this out. Can I ask you to listen while I try, and we can open the conversation from there?

And always, acknowledge them for bravely holding your story while you share. You could say something as simple as...

Thank you so much for letting me share this with you. I am working really hard to heal the remnants I've been holding onto, and this has been really hard. It means so much that I have a safe space with you to open myself up and know I'm seen and heard through the lens of love.

Chapter 8: How Do I Trust Again?

If you're a people-pleaser, recovering or otherwise, it may support you to ask yourself a series of questions when making decisions as a way to sharpen your trust muscle. I've found that getting quiet, and feeling into the body, naming the sensations and where they're felt, is a powerful way to find your truest self again.

Then ask yourself:

1. Once I've made my decision, how do I want to feel?
2. Does this decision bring me closer or farther away from my desired state (peace, joy, etc.)?
3. Would choosing something different feel better, more aligned?
4. What am I afraid will happen if I make the "wrong" decision?
5. Am I willing to bet on myself and lean into self-trust in this moment as a practice to gain the confidence I crave for my decisions moving forward?

Then act accordingly. Trust is earned. That includes the trust we have with ourselves. Just as with a loved one, when *we* break that trust, it's up to *us* to repair it. And to do so takes intentional action, compassion, and a whole lotta love.

Be gentle with yourself and your process. Remember that it's yours, and how you choose to repair it is in your hands (and heart).

Here are some questions to consider regarding intimacy, which does not necessarily mean sex...

1. What are some ways you can support yourself to feel more empowered?
2. What are some coping skills that have worked well for you?
3. What can you put in place to help you remember to use these skills as needed?
4. What positive qualities did you develop in response to managing a traumatic life event, possibly in which you didn't choose to participate but happened to you anyway?
5. How can these skills help you in the present and future?

Here are some questions to consider as you explore your own sexuality and capacity for intimacy...

1. Where on/in your body can you touch and, in turn, feel positive sensations?
2. What are you still not allowing yourself to experience?
3. What do you need to release to feel safe in your body and during sexual encounters, both with self and partnered?
4. What is working well for you in terms of healing your relationship with your body?
5. If partnered, what fears/desires do you want to share with them to create a deeper connection?
6. What are your fears in doing so?
7. Are you willing to release these fears, and re-commit to your sexual liberation/freedom?
8. If not, why?

In my Somatic Trauma Therapy Certification training, one of our instructors, Staci K. Haines, author of *The Politics of Trauma: Somatics, Healing and Social Justice*, shared this consent practice with us, and I wanted to pass it along to you in case it supports you on your journey as well.

In any given situation you have agency to say a *centered yes, centered maybe,* or *centered no* based on what's important to you—instead of deferring to an automatic response based on conditioning or past experiences/responses. Use this exercise to establish boundaries that feel aligned in your body.

1. Seated or standing, relax your jaw, your eyeballs, your shoulders and all your limbs.
2. Let your breath relax all the way down your spine.
3. Choose a person or situation that you want to practice boundaries with (this is imperative for this exercise).
4. Notice your body sensations: temperature, any pressure, tightness, etc.
5. Place one foot in front of the other, then extend your arms out straight in front of you (this is a "no"). Now place your arms in front of you, with your hands below waist, palms down (this is a "maybe"). Now place your legs side-by-side, with your palms up, and your arms down at a diagonal by your side (this is a "yes").
6. How does each position feel in your body? Be honest with yourself.

This practice allows for *choice* vs. jumping into a reactive response, and may support you as you navigate your own boundaries with a new sense of confidence.

Chapter 9: Will I Ever Feel Safe to Let Love In?

If you notice yourself seeking "love" outside of yourself, ask yourself:

1. What am I hiding from?
2. Why is the idea of disconnecting from the external world to be with myself in silence/stillness so uncomfortable?
3. Who am I without all of the noise (distraction)?
4. Am I willing to get quiet enough to listen and honor what I truly need and want?

Chapter 10: What Was It For?

This was the hardest question for me. While it became clear pretty quickly that my assault was tied to the work I was put in the world to do, I still held onto my pain as a way to make the story real and validate the choices I was making.

I encourage you to sit with this question with an open heart. Ask yourself, *Does it really matter why it happened?* And if the answer is yes, then start to look at your journey from the moment your trauma occurred until now. I am willing to bet you will begin to see some patterns that have led you to people and experiences that may never have happened otherwise. You may even find that you've changed in ways that have allowed you to be more compassionate and kind toward adversity—I see this one a lot.

List the lessons or themes you've noticed, and after each one write, *Thank you.*

Gratitude turns what we have (and what we've been through) into enough. This does not say that what happened was okay. What it does say, however, is that you have survived even your worst days which tells me, you can get through this too.

Closure

Here are a couple practices I learned from one of my energy healers, Rebecca, to help you close the gap and release any stagnant energy that may be lingering so that you can heal, fully and completely.

Candle Closure Ceremony

This simple practice can be so powerful so even if it seems silly or strange, I'm inviting you to try something new, out of your comfort zone, and remain open. The worst that can happen is…nothing. So go for it! Say *yes* to possibility, warrior.

1. State your intention. *(What do you want to let go of? Heal?)*
2. Take two small-ish candles (tall/thin or birthday candles will work, too) and place them next to each other; one is *you*, the other is the *story* you can't seem to let go of.
3. Then tie a thin string around the candles to connect them at the midway point and light the candles, allowing them to burn and sever their tie to each other.
4. State your intention again, although now in present-tense. *(i.e. I am free of my story)*
5. Now go be free, warrior. And live the life waiting for you.

Write a Closure Letter

This can be to a person, experience, whatever you're holding onto that you want to release. Be intentional. Just as with the candle ceremony above, the idea is for you to be honest and vulnerable with yourself and allow yourself to let go. It doesn't have to be long, or complicated. Let it be whatever it is.

Here's the one I wrote:

Dear rape,

I now release the vow I made, to use my pain for a purpose for all of my days. I did what I said I would do (create positive change), and now I am ready to close this chapter and move on to my next mission. I am proud of the way I showed up to help myself and others heal.

Thank you.
I am now complete.

I love you,
Sheree

Acknowledgments

You hear it all the time when it comes to parenting, *it takes a village.* Well, the same goes for writing—*and finishing*—a book! For years, I stopped and started, never quite feeling like the timing was right. Little did I know it wasn't the timing I was holding out for, but the courage necessary to go all in. The support I've had from my incredible team gave me the courage I needed, which made birthing this book possible. The world is a better place because of the kind and generous hearts of the people named below. Thank you for believing in me.

Huge thanks to **Jessica Brown**, my *proofreader* (also an amazing non-fiction book editor) for being willing to be the first set of eyes on my full manuscript. Your honest feedback provided the permission I didn't know I needed to keep going, especially when it felt hard. Thank you for the work you do in the world, and for helping me bring my book to life.

Deep gratitude to **Christy Carlson**, my brilliant *editor* for tenderly holding my story with such care and compassion. Your constant support, encouragement and honesty helped transform this book into something so much bigger (and more meaningful) than I could've ever imagined. You reflected back the very purpose and intention I had for sharing my story with such kindness, giving me a boost in confidence along the way, as well as a loving kick in the ass when needed. Thank you for seeing me, and supporting me in creating something worth sharing so publicly.

An enormous thank you to my friends and partners at **Author's Unite** for holding my hand through the *publishing process* including: cover design, formatting, publication and distribution. Too many stories are left in the ethers *unheard*, because of this last—often frustrating and tedious—step. Thank you for making my dream of releasing my story into the world a reality. You were the final piece needed on this long, and vulnerable journey home to myself.

Resources

Libby Carstensen

Grief and Loss Coach, Yoga and Breathwork Instructor

Her 8-week grief program helped my healing tremendously.
Find more information: www.libbyc.com.

Healing Modalities to Consider

Eye Movement Desensitization and Reprocessing (EMDR)
Somatic Experiencing (SE)
Cognitive Behavioral Therapy (CBT)
Narrative Exposure Therapy (NET)
Psychodynamic Trauma Therapy
Internal Family Systems (IFS)
Acceptance and Commitment Therapy (ACT)
Yoga and Mindfulness

Books to Consider

The Body Keeps the Score by Bessel van der Kolk
Childhood Disrupted by Donna Jackson Nakazawa
In An Unspoken Voice by Peter A. Levine
The Empath's Survival Guide by Judith Orloff
Attached by Amir Levine and Rachel Heller
Becoming the One by Sheleana Aiyana

About the Author

Sheree Trask is an Author, seasoned Ghostwriter, and Nonfiction Book Writing Coach. She supports coaches, healers, and transformational leaders ready to write their transformational book so they can make a bigger impact, build authority and be recognized as a leader in their field. Sheree has ghostwritten books for some of the most influential names in the personal development and holistic health space, having her work published with Hay House, Inc. in 2018. She is on a mission to help transform the hearts and minds of humanity through courageous storytelling so that together, we can raise the collective consciousness of our world and truly be free to live—*unapologetically out loud.*

Learn more at www.shereetrask.com.

About the Author

Made in the USA
Middletown, DE
13 October 2022